KEYS

Of the Kingdom of

HEAVEN

AND

Power thereof, according to the

WORD of GOD

BY

That Learned and Judicious Divine
Mr JOHN COTTON, Teacher of the Church

At *Boston* in *New England*

Tending to reconcile some present differences about

DISCIPLINE

Genesis 13:7-8. *And Abraham said unto Lot, let there be no strife, I pray between thee, and me; for we be brethren.*

Genesis 45:24. *And Joseph said to his Brethren (when they were going the third time out of Egypt) see that ye fall not out by the way.*

Acts 7:26. *Sirs, ye be Brethren, why do ye wrong one to another?*

Ephesians 4:15. *αληθεύοντε ἐν ἀγάπη αὐξήσωμεν εἰ αὐτόν & c.*

Contents

Preface.

Of the Keys of the Kingdom of Heaven.

Preface

This reprint of the original work of 'The Keys' by Mr John Cotton, has sought to be sensitive to the original work and to the era that we now live in; by updating on a few occasions archaic words. Thus giving us today a work that remains true to its original (without changing sentences or meanings), but readily useable for today's church. There have been numbers inserted into brackets e.g. **(1)** so that the reader can refer to the index at the back of this book. This we hope will bring many into contact for the first time with the writings of Mr John Cotton and the works that he had accomplished while he laboured for the Lord.

Editor

P. Joseph

Life Sketch of Mr John Cotton.

John Cotton (an English and American Puritan divine) was born on December 4th, 1584 in Derby, England. He was the son of Roland Cotton, a lawyer who was both godly and wealthy, enough so to provide his son with a good education. He entered and was educated at Trinity College Cambridge (when being just thirteen years of age, a boy much advanced for his young age). Graduating with a B.A. in 1603 and M.A. in 1606. He became a fellow in Emmanuel College Cambridge in about 1607, (then a stronghold of Puritanism), where during the next six years he became Dean; also being an effective tutor, lecturer and catechist and preaching occasionally at St Mary's Church, (whilst in his studies, he became a great student in the ancient Biblical languages). It was during this time when his conscience was awakened (he suppressed and resisted the preaching of William Perkins). But he came under the preaching of Richard Sibbes whose preaching awakened his soul to show him his lost condition (this changed his preaching, and it became more obvious to his hearers of this spiritual change).

He was ordained Priest and Deacon on July 13th, 1610 at Lincoln. Then on June 24th, 1612 he became vicar of the parish church of St Botolphs in Boston, Lincolnshire (when he was still only twenty-seven years of age), there he remained for twenty-one years and became extremely popular with his congregation. In 1613 he received his B.D. Becoming more and more a Puritan in spirit, he ceased, about 1615, to observe certain Anglican ceremonies prescribed by the legally authorized ritual. He attracted those of Puritan sympathies during his time in Boston; a John Preston who was converted under the ministry of Cotton, sent his divinity students to complete their preparation for the ministry with Cotton. William Ames sent some German students to Cotton from the Netherlands. Puritans of all shades came to hear and speak with him, Archbishop Ussher being a more notable one. Boston as well as spiritually prospering under this ministry; also prospered in secular concernments, becoming a prosperous town, where many came to reside. In September of 1630, his wife Elizabeth (Horrocks) and Cotton himself were stricken down with ague (an acute/malarial fever). His wife died through this and Cotton was laid down for about a year.

It was during his time of recuperation that he became acquainted with the colonization of New England. His interest had already been aroused when he preached a farewell sermon in Southampton in March of 1630. On the 6th of April of 1632 he married again a Sarah Hawkridge (widow of William Story). Not long after this he was summoned to the Court of High Commission of William Laud. On hearing this he fled to London to go into hiding in the autumn of that year self same year. During his time in London, several Puritans seeking to persuade him from his nonconformity and anticipated journey to New England visited him. On this he reasoned with John Davenport, Thomas Goodwin and Philip Nye on nonconformity and these men were eventually persuaded of Independency (Congregationalism).

It was from his hiding that he decided to immigrate to the colony of Massachusetts Bay, New England with his wife; going with him were Thomas Hooker and Samuel Stone. They set sail in July of 1633 on the Griffin bound for their new land, arriving at Boston early in September. On arrival, Cotton was warmly welcomed and accepted into this new land. (*Boston was founded on September 17, 1630, on a peninsula called Shawmut by its original Native American inhabitants. The peninsula was connected to the mainland by a narrow isthmus, and surrounded by the waters of Massachusetts Bay and the marshes at the mouth of the Charles River. Boston's early European settlers first called the area Trimountain. They later renamed the town for Boston, England, in Lincolnshire, from which several prominent colonists emigrated notably John Cotton*).

It was not long before the Lord started to use his services. For on the 10th of October of 1633 Cotton was chosen and ordained "Teacher" of the First Church of Boston, of which John Wilson (1588-1667) was pastor, (he remained there until his death on the 23rd of December 1652). He was greatly used in the religious and political life of Boston and the surrounding New England territories, his work also having effect abroad and in particular on the shores of England. He conformed for the time being to the practices of the church. But he had his own reservations and kept working away until he could work out that ideal model of church government (Congregationalism). He managed to minister within the

Anglican ecclesiology for some twenty-one years and remain a nonconformist, therefore he could sit tight until such time that his thoughts and studies would come into more public light and agreement, (*he would spend up to twelve hours a day in his studies*). During his years in Boston he became involved in such controversies as antinomianism, where he defended a Calvinistic position and eventually this led to the banishment of Mrs Anne Hutchinson who espoused those antinomian views. He was also engaged in written controversy with Roger Williams over questions on church membership and the civil magistrate's power over the church.

During his ministry in Boston many came to hear him and thus many were added to the church. In 1642 he with some others were invited to attend the gathering in London of which would become to be known as the Westminster Assembly. The other men invited from New England were Thomas Hooker from Connecticut and John Davenport from New Haven. They never attended the Assembly, but Cotton tried much to influence the Assembly on the side of the Independents with his writing on Congregational polity. This brought about a few publications: *The Way of the Churches in New England and The Keys of the Kingdom of Heaven. The Way of the Churches in New England* was written before The Keys but published afterward (1645). The Keys was published in (1644). In 1648 Cotton published *The Way of Congregational Churches Cleared*, in answer to his opponents in England. He had come to his ideal in church polity after those years spent in diligent study; he was now defending this ideal. Cotton declared no total independence, as with Brownism of the day, (*The Brownists were a movement formed on a theory of union published by the theologian <u>Robert Browne</u> in 1592 and arising from the <u>Nonconformist</u> religious movement in England during the <u>Puritan</u> reformation*); nor total Presbyterianism, which prevailed at the Westminster Assembly. It never went as far as Brown because it never advocated the total separation of Congregations (of those of like mind). This was a statement that would characterise a Church from both, Presbyterianism and Brownism. It came as a middle way between both. He was backed up in the Assembly by the Independents (Congregationalists): Thomas Goodwin, Philip Nye, Jeremiah Burroughs,

William Bridge and Sadrach Simpson were men of like mind who attended the Assembly.

In 1648 he was appointed along with Richard Mather and Ralph Partridge by the Cambridge Synod (New England) to draw up a model for Church Government. The result being the Cambridge Platform of 1649, being presented to the Massachusetts General Court. The Cambridge Platform is the definitive statement of church order and discipline which was produced by the Congregationalists of New England.

It was Cotton's writing's on church government (*The Keys of the Kingdom of Heaven*), that persuaded the Calvinist theologian John Owen to separate from the Presbyterian church, after which he became very influential in the development of Congregationalist theology and ideas of church government.

It was whilst preaching to his students at Harvard in 1652, that Cotton caught a cold, which became an inflammation of the lungs. This was now the end for Cotton, for he preached his last sermon on November 21st, 1652, a few days later dying of asthma on the 23rd of December.

TO THE READER

THE greatest commotions in Kingdoms have for the most part been raised and maintained for and about *Power*, and *Liberties*, of the *Rulers* and the *Ruled*, together with the due bounds and limits of either: And the like has fallen out in Churches, and is continued to this day in the sharpest contentions (though now the seat of the war is changed) who should be the *first* adequate, and the complete *subject* of that *Church-power,* which Christ has left on earth; *how bounded,* and *to whom committed.* This controversy is in a special manner the lot of these present times: And now that most parties (that can pretend any thing towards it) have in several ages had their turns and vicissitudes of so long a possession of it, and their plans for their sever all pretences; have been so much and so long heard, it may well be hoped it is near determining; and that Christ will shortly settle this power upon the right heirs, to whom he primitively did bequeath it.

In those former darker times, this golden Ball was thrown up by the *Clergy* (so-called) alone to run for among themselves: And as they quietly possessed the name κληρός. The *Clergy*, and of the *Church*, appropriated to themselves; so answerably all manner of interest in power or cognisance of matters of the Church, was wholly left and quitted to them: while the *People that* then *knew not the Law,* having given up their souls to an implicit faith in what was to be believed, did much more suffer themselves to be deprived of all Liberties in Church-affairs. This royal donation bestowed by Christ upon his Church, was taken up and placed in so high thrones of Bishops, Popes, General Counsels, & c. Not only *far above these things on earth,* the people; but *things in Heaven* also, we mean the *Angels* and *Ministers* of the Churches themselves; in so great a remoteness from the *people,* that the least right or interest therein, was no so much as suspected to belong to them. But towards these later times, after many removals of it down again, and this at the issue of many suits again and again renewed and removed, and upon the sentence (even of whole States) as often reversed. It has now in these days been brought so near unto the people, that *they* also have begun to plead and sue for a portion, and legacy bequeathed them in it.

The *Saints* (in these knowing times) finding that the *Key of knowledge* has so far opened their hearts, that they see with their own eyes into the substantials of Godliness, and that through the instruction and guidance of their teachers, they are enabled to understand for themselves such other things as they are to enjoin in the practice of. They do therefore further (many of them) begin more then to suspect, that some share in the *Key of Power* should likewise appertain unto them.

It was the unhappiness of those, who first in these later times received this plea of the peoples right, to ere on the other extreme (as it has ever been the fate of truth, when it first arises in the Church from under that long night of darkness which Antichristianism had brought upon the world, to have a long shadow of error to accompany it) by laying the plea and claim on their behalf unto the *whole* power; and that the *Elders* set over them did but exercise that power for them, which was properly theirs, and which Christ had (as they contended) radically and originally stated in the people only.

But after that all titles have been pleaded, of those that are content with nothing but the whole, the final judgement and sentence may (possibly) fall to be a suitable and due proportioned *distribution and dispersion of this power* into several interests, and the whole to neither part. In *Commonwealths,* it is a *Dispersion* of several portions of power and rights into several hands, jointly to concur and agree in acts and process of weight and moment, which causes that healthful κράσις and constitution of them, which makes them lasting, and preserves their peace, when none of all sorts find they are excluded, but as they have a share of concernments, so that a fit measure of power or privilege is left and betrusted to them. And accordingly the wisdom of the first Constitutors of Commonwealths is most seen in such a just balancing of power and privileges, and besides also in setting the exact limits of that which is committed unto each; yes, and is more admired by us in this than their other Laws; and in experience, a clear and distinct definement and confinement of all such parcels of power, both for the kind and extent of them, is judged to be as essentially necessary (if not more) than whatever other statutes, that set out the kinds and degrees of *crimes* or *penalties*.

So in that *Polity* or Government by which Christ would have his *Churches* ordered, the right *disposal of* the power therein (we humbly suppose) may lie in a due and proportioned *allotment and dispersion* (though not in the same measure and degree) into several hands, according unto the several concernments and interests that each rank in his Church may have; rather than in an entire and sole trust committed to any one man (though never so able) or any one sort of kind of men of Officers, although diversified into never so many subordinations under one another. And in like manner, we cannot but imagine, that Christ has been as exact in setting forth the true bounds and limits of whatever portion of power he has imparted unto any (if we of this age could attain rightly to discern it) as he has been in ordering what kind of censures, and for what sins and what degrees of proceedings unto those censures; which we find he has been punctual in.

Now the scope which this grave and judicious Author in this Treatise does pursue, is, to lay forth the just lines and terriers of this division of *Church-power,* unto all the several subjects of it; to the end to allay the contentions now on foot, about it. And in general he lays this fundamental *Maxine,* that holds in common true to all particulars, to whom any portion of power can be supposed to be committed: *That look whatever power or right any of the possessors and subjects of it may have, they have it each alike immediately* (that is, in respect of a mediation *delegation* or *dependence* on each other) *from Christ,* and so are *each, the first subjects of that power that is allotted to them.* And for the particular subjects themselves, he follows that division (in the handling of them) which the Controversy itself has made unto his hands; that is to say: 1. *What power each* single *Congregation* (which is endowed with a Charter to be body-politique to Christ) has granted to it to exercise within itself: And 2. *What measure,* or rather, kind of power Christ has placed in *Neighbour-Churches* without it, and in *association* with it.

For the first. As he supposes each Congregation such, as to have the privilege of enjoining it *Presbytery,* or company of more or less *Elders,* proper unto itself; so being thus Presbyerated, be asserted this incorporate body of society to be the *first* and *primary* subject of a complete and entire power within itself over its own members; yes, and the *sole native subject* of the power of *Ordination* and *Excommunication,* which is the highest Censure. And whereas this corporation consists both of *Elders* and *Brethren,* (for as for women and children, there is special exception by a *Statute-Law* of Christ against their enjoinment of any part of this public power); His scope is to demonstrate a distinct and several share and interest of power, in matters of common concernment, vouchsafed to each of these, and dispersed among both, by Charter from the Lord; as in some of our *Towns corporate,* to a company of *Aldermen,* the Rulers, and a *Common-Council,* a body of the people, there uses to be the like: He giving unto the *Elders* or *Presbytery* a binding power of *Rule* and *Authority* proper and peculiar unto them; and unto the *Brethren,* distinct and apart, an interest of *power* and *privilege* to concurre with them, and that such affairs should not be transacted, but with the joint agreement of both, though out of a different right; so that as a Church of *Brethren* only, could not proceed to any public censures, without they have *Elders* over them, so nor in the Church have the *Elders* power to censure without the concurrence of the people; and likewise so, as each *alone* has not power of Excommunication the whole of either, though *Together* they have power over any particular person or persons in each.

And because these particular Congregations, both *Elders* and *People,* may disagree and miscarry, and abuse this power committed to them; He therefore, secondly, asserts an association or communion of Churches, sending their *Elders* and *Messengers* into a Synod, (so he properly chooses to style those *Assemblies* of *Elders* which the *Reformed Churches* do call *Classes* or *Presbyteries,* that so he might distinguish them from those *Presbyteries* of *Congregations* before mentioned). And acknowledges that it is an *Ordinance* of *Christ,* unto whom Christ has (in relation to rectifying *Mal-administrations* and *healing dissentions* in particular *Congregations,* and the like cases) committed a due and just measure of power, suited and proportioned to those ends; and furnished them, not only with *ability* to give *counsel* and *advice,* but further upon such occasions with a *Ministerial power* and *authority* to *determine, declare* and *enjoin* such things as may tend to the reducing such

Congregations to right order and peace. Only in his bounding and defining this *power,* he affirms it to be: First, for the *kind* and *quality* of it, but a *dogmatical* or *doctrinal power,* (though stamped with authority Ministerial as an *Ordinance* of Christ) whether in judging of Controversies of faith, and (when they disturb the peace of particular *Congregations,* and which themselves find too difficult for them) or in discerning matters of fact, and what confines they do deserve: but not armed with authority and power of *Excommunicating* or delivering *unto Satan,* either the *Congregations* or the *Members* of them: But they in such cases, having declared and judged the nature of the offence, and admonished the peccant *Churches,* and discerned what they ought to do with their offending members; they are to leave the *formal act* of this censure to that authority which can only execute it, placed by Christ in those *Churches* themselves; which if they deny to do, or profit in their miscarriage, then to determine to *withdraw communion from them.* And also for the extent of this power in such *Assemblies* and *Association* of *Churches,* be limits and confines, *that* also unto cases, and with cautions (which will appear in the *Discourse*) that is to say, that they should not entrench or impair the privilege of entire Jurisdiction committed unto each *Congregation*, (as a liberty purchased them by Christ's blood) but to leave them free to the exercise and use of it, until they abuse that power, or are able to manage it; and in that case only to assist, guide, and direct them, and not take on them to administer it from them, but with them, and by them.

As for ourselves, we are yet, neither afraid, nor ashamed to make profession (in the midst of all the high waves on both sides dashing on us) that the substance of this brief *Extract* from the *Authors* larger *Discourse,* is, that very *Middle-way* (which in our Apology we did in the general intimate and intend) between that which is called *Brownism,* and the *Presbyterian-government,* as it is practiced; whereof the one does in effect put the chief (if not the whole) of the rule and government unto the hands of the people, and drowns the *Elders* votes (who are but a few) in the major part of theirs; And the other, taking the chief and the principal parts of that rule (which we conceive is the due of each *Congregation,* the *Elders* and *Brethren*) into this jurisdiction of a common *Presbytery* of several *Congregations,* does thereby in like manner swallow up, not only the interests of the people, but even the votes of the *Elders* of that *Congregation* concerned, in the major part of it.

Neither let it seem arrogance in us, but a testimony rather to the truth, further to Remonstrate, that this very *Boundary platform* and *disposement* of *Church-power,* as here it is (we speak for the substance of it) let out and stated; as also that the tenure and exercise of it in all these subjects, should be immediate from Christ unto them all, is not now new unto our thoughts; yes it is no other than what many of our friends, and some that are of a different opinion, having known our private judgements long, as likewise own Notes and transcripts written long ago, can testify; besides many public profession since as occasion has been offered: Insomuch as when we first read this of this learned Author (knowing what has been the more general current, both of the practice and judgement of our *Brethren* for the Congregational way) we confess we were filled with wonderment at that Divine and, that had thus led the judgements (without the least mutual interchange or intimation of thoughts or notions in these particulars) of our *Brethren* there, and our selves (unworthy to be mentioned with them) here. Only we crave leave of the reverend Author, and those *Brethren* that had the view of it, to declare: that we assent not to all expressions scattered up and down, or all and every Assertion interwoven in it; yes, nor to all the grounds or allegations of Scriptures; nor should we in all things perhaps have used the same terms to express the same materials by.

For instance, we humbly conceive *Prophesying* (as the Scripture terms it) or speaking to the edification of the whole Church may (sometimes) be performed by Brethren gifted, though not in the Office as Elders of the Church, only. 1. Occasionally, not in an ordinary course. 2. By men of such abilities as are fit for Office: And. 3. Not assuming this of themselves, but judges such by those that have the power, and so allowed and designed to it: And. 4. So as their Doctrine be subjected (for the *judging of it*) in an especial manner: the *Teaching Elders* of that Church: And when it is thus cautioned, we see no more incongruity for such to speak to a point of Divinity in a Congregation, then for men of like abilities to speak to, and debate of matters of Religion in an

Assembly of Divines, which this reverend Author allows; and here, with us, is practised.

Again, in all humility, we yet see not that Assembly of *Apostles, Elders, and Brethren (Acts 15),* to have been a *formal Synod,* of Messengers, sent out of a set and combined association from neighbour Churches; but an Assembly of the *Church of Jerusalem,* and of the Messengers from the *Church of Antioch* alone; that were far remote each from other, and electively now met: Nor are we for the present convinced that the *Apostles* to the end to make this a Precedent of such a *formal Synod*, did act therein as Ordinary *Elders,* and not out of Apostolical guidance and assistance; But we rather conceive (if we would simply consider mutual aspects which these two Churches and their *Elders* stood in this conjunction, abstracting from them that influence and improffesion which (that superior Sphere) the Apostles who were then present had in this transaction) this to have been a *Consultation* (as the learned Author does also acknowledge it to have been in its first original, only rising up to be a General Council by the Apostles presence, they being *Elders* of all the Churches); or if you will, a reference by way of *Arbitration* for deciding of that great Controversy risen amongst them at *Antioch*, which they found to be too difficult for themselves; and so to be a warrant indeed for all such ways of communion between all, or any, especially neighbour Churches; and upon like occasions to be Ordinances furnished with Ministerial power for such ends and purposes. Our reasons for this, we are now many ways bound up from giving the account of, in this way, and at this season; But however, if it should have been so intended as the learned Author judges, and the *Apostles* to have acted therein as ordinary *Elders*, yet the lines of that proportion of power that could be drawn from that pattern, would extend no further than a Ministerial Doctrinal power, & c. in such Assemblies, which we willingly grant. And it may be observed with what a wary eye and exact aim he takes the latitude and elevation of that power there held forth, not daring to attribute the least, either for kind of degree, then what that example warrants, which was at utmost but a doctrinal discernment both of the truth of that controversy they were consulted in; as also the matter of fact in those that had taught contrary, as beliers of them, and subverters of the faith; without so much as brandishing the sword and power of

15

Excommunication, against those high and gross delinquents, or others, that should not obey them in that Epistle.

Only in the last place, for the further clearing the difference of the peoples interest (which the reverend Author usually calls *Liberty,* sometimes *Power*) and the *Elders rule and authority* (which makes that *first distribution* of Church-power *in particular Congregations*) is likewise for the illustration of that other allotment of *Ministerial doctrinal power* in an association or communion of Churches as served from the power of *Excommunication* (which is *the second*). We take the boldness to cast a weak beam of our dim light upon either of these; and to present how these have lain stated in our thoughts, to this end that we may haply prevent some readers' mistake, especially about the former. For the first, we conceive the *Elders* and *Brethren* in each Congregation as they are usually in the New Testament thus mentioned distinctly apart, and this when their meeting together is spoken of, so they make in each Congregation, two distinct interests (though meeting in one Assembly) as the interest of the *Common-Council* or body of the people, in some *Corporations*, is distinct from that of the company of *Aldermen*; so as without the consent and concurrence of both nothing is esteemed as a Church act. But so as in this company of *Elders,* this power is properly *Authority;* but in the people there is *privilege* or *power.* An apparent difference between these two is evident to us by this: That two or three, or more select persons should be put into an Office, and be trusted with an entire interest of power for a multitude, to which that multitude ought (by a command from Christ) to be subject and obedient as to an ordinance to guide them in their consent, and in whole sentence the ultimate formal Ministerial act of binding and loosing should consist: this power must needs be esteemed and acknowledged in these few to have the proper notion and character of *Authority*, in comparison of that power (which must yet concurre with theirs) that is in a whole body or multitude of men, who have a greater and nearer interest and concernment in those affairs, over which these few are set as Rulers.

This difference of power does easily appear in comparing the several interests of *Father* and *Child,* in his disposement of her in marriage, and her concurrence with him therein, (although we intend not the parallel between the things themselves). *A Virgin daughter* has a *power* truly and properly so called, yes, and a power ultimately to dissent upon an unsatisfied dislike; yes, and it must be an act of her consent, that makes the marriage valid: But yet, for her Parents to have a power to guide her in her choice (which she ought in duty to obey) and a power which must also concur to bestow her, or the marriage is invalid, this (comparing her interest (wherein she is more nearly and intimately concerned) with theirs) does arise to the notion of an *extrinsical authority*; whereas that power which is in her, is but simply the power of her own act, in which her own concernment does interest her free by an *intrinsical right*. The like difference would appear if we had seen a Government tempered of an *Aristocracy* and *Democracy;* in which, suppose the people have a share, and their actual consent is necessary to all laws and sentences, whereas a few Nobles that are set over them (whose concernment is less general) in whom the formal *sanction* of all should lie, in these it were *Rule* and *Authority*, in that multitude but *Power* and *interest;* and such an Authority is to be given to a Presbytery of Elders in a particular Congregation, or else (as we have long since been resolved), all that is said in the New Testament about their *Rule*, and of the peoples *Obedience* to them, is to be looked upon but as Metaphors, and to hold no proportion with any substantial reality of Rule and Government.

And in this Distribution of power, Christ has had a suitable and due regard unto the estate and condition of his Church, as now under the New Testament, he has qualified and dignified it. Under the Old Testament, it was in its infancy, but it is comparatively come forth of its nonage, and grown up to a riper age (both as the tenure of the Covenant of Grace in difference from the old, runs in the Prophets, and as *Paul* to the *Galatians* expresses it). They are therefore more generally able, if visible Saints (which is to be the subject matter of Churches under the New Testament) to join with their Guides and Leaders in judging and discerning what concerns their own and their *Brethrens* consciences; and therefore Christ has not now lodged the sole power of all Church matters solely and entirely in the Churches *Tutors* and *Governors*, as of old when it was under age he did: But yet because of their weakness and unskillfulness (for the generality of them) in comparison to those whom he has ascended to give gifts unto, on purpose for their guidance and the government of them; He has therefore placed a Rule and Authority in those Officers over them, not directing only, but binding: so as not only nothing (in an ordinary way of Church-government) should be done without them, but not esteemed validly done unless done by them. And thus by means of this due and golden balancing and poising of power and interest, Authority and Privilege, in *Elders* and the *Brethren*, this Government might neither degenerate into Lordliness and oppression in Rulers over the Flock, as not having all power in their hands alone; nor yet into Anarchy and confusion in the Flock among themselves; and so as all things belonging to men's consciences might be transacted to common edification, and satisfaction.

For the second, let it not seem a Paradox that a *Ministerial Doctrinal* authority should be found served from that power of *Excommunication*, to second it, if not obeyed. Every Minister and Pastor has in himself, alone a Ministerial Doctrinal authority over the whole Church that is in his charge, and every person in it, to instruct, *rebuke, exhort with all authority*: By reason of which, those under him are bound to obey him in The Lord, not only in *vi materae*, by virtue of the matter of the commands, in that they are commands of Christ (for so he should speak with no more authority than any other man; yes, a *Child*, who speaking a truth out of the Word, should *lead us,* as the Prophet speaks); But further, by reason of that Ministerial authority which Christ has endowed him withal, he is to be looked at by them as an Ordinance of *His*, over them and towards them: And yet he alone has not the authority of Excommunication *in him,* to enforce his Doctrine, if any do again say it: Neither therefore is this authority (as in him considered) to be judged vain and fruitless and ineffectual, to draw men to obedience.

Neither let it seem strange, that the power of this Censure, of cutting men off, and *Delivering them to Satan* (in which the positive part (*and indeed the controversy between us and others*), of *Excommunication* lies) should be inseparably linked by Christ unto a particular Congregation, as the proper native privilege of this, so as that no Assembly or Company of *Elders* justly presumed and granted to be more wise and judicious, should assume it to themselves, or sever the formal power of it from the particular Congregations. For though it be hard to give reason of Christ's institutions; yet there is usually in the ways of human wisdom and reason, something analogous thereunto, which may serve to illustrate, if not to justify this *dispersion of interests*: And so (if we mistake not) there be found even of this wisdom of our Ancestors, in the constitutions of this Kingdom; *The sentencing to death* of any subject in the kingdom, as it is the highest civil punishment, so of all other the nearest and exact parallel to this in spirituals, of cutting a soul off, and delivering it to Satan; yet the power of this high judgement is not put into the hands of an Assembly of Lawyers only, no, not of all the Judges themselves, men selected for wisdom, faithfulness, and gravity who yet are by office designed to have an interest herein; But when they upon any special Cause of difficulty, for counsel and direction in such judgements do all meet, (as sometimes they do) yet they have not power to pronounce this sentence of death upon any man, without the concurrence of a Jury of his Peers, which are of his own rank: and in Corporations, of such as are Inhabitants of the same place: And with a Jury of these (men, of themselves not supposed to be so skilful in the Laws etc.) two judges, yes, one, with other Justices on the Bench, has power to adjudge and pronounce that which all of them, and all the Lawyers in this kingdom together, have not without a Jury. And we of this nation use to admire the care and wisdom of our Ancestors herein, and do esteem this privilege of the Subject in this particular (peculiar to our Nation) as one of the glories of our Laws, and do make boast of it as such a liberty and security to each persons life, as (we think) no Nation about us can show the like. And what should be the reason of such a constitution but this (which in the beginning we insisted on) the dispersion of power into several hands, which in capital matters, every man's trial should run through; whereof the one should have the tie of like common interest to oblige them unto faithfulness; as the other should have skill and wisdom to guide them and direct therein.

And besides that interest that is in any kind of Association, fraternity, yes, or neighbourhood, or like wise, that which is from the common case of men alike subjected to an Authority set over them to sentence them; there is also the special advantage of an exact knowledge of the fact in the heinous circumstances of it, yes, and (in these cases) of the ordinary conversation of the person offending.

We need not enlarge the application of this: Although a greater *Assembly of Elders* are to be reverenced as more wise and able, than a few *Elders* with their single *Congregations*, and accordingly may have higher doctrinal power, (a power properly, and peculiarly suited to their abilities) in cases of difficulty, to determine and direct Congregations in their way; yet Christ has not betrusted them with that power He has done the Congregations; because they are abstracted from the people: And so *one Tribe* of men concerned in all the forementioned respects *is wanting*, which Christ would have personally concurring, not by delegation or representation alone, not to the *execution* only, but even to the *legal sentence* also of *cutting men off*, as in the former parallel and instance may be observed. Yes, and the higher and the greater the association of the *Presbyteries* are, the further are they removed from *the people*, and although you might have thereby a greater help, in that *Judicial* knowledge of the *Rule*, to be proceeded by: yet they are in a further distance (and disenabled thereby) from that precise *practique* knowledge of the *Fact* and frame of *spirit* in the person transgressing. And cases may be as truly difficult and hard to be decided from obscurity and want of light into the Circumstantiation of the Fact, and person, in which it was committed, and by him obstinately persisted in; as the Law itself.

Other considerations of like weight might be here added, if not for the proof (which we do not here intend) yet the clearing of this particular: As also to demonstrate that *that* other way proceeding by *withdrawing communion* is most suitable to the relation, that by Christ's endowment, all Churches stand in one towards another; yes, and wherein the least (being a body of Christ) does stand unto all: But we should too much exceed the bounds of an Epistle, and too long detain the Reader from the fruitful and pregnant labours of the worthy Author.

The God of Peace and Truth, Sanctify all the truths in it, to all those holy ends (and through his Grace much more), which the holy and peaceable spirit of the Author did intend.

By THOMAS GOODWIN

& PHILIP NYE.

Of the Keys of the Kingdom of Heaven, and the Power thereof; according to the Word of God

CHAPTER 1

What the Keys of the Kingdom of Heaven be, and what their Power.

The Keys of the Kingdom of Heaven are promised by the Lord Jesus (the Head and King of His Church) unto Peter (Matthew 16:19). *To thee* (says Christ) *will I give the Keys of the Kingdom of Heaven: and whatsoever thou shalt bind on earth, shall be bound in heaven; and whatsoever thou shalt loose on earth, shall be loosed in Heaven.* The words being allegorical are therefore somewhat obscure: and holding forth honour and power in the church, are therefore controversial; for where there is no honour (nor pride to pursue it) there is no contention. It will not therefore be amiss, for opening of the Doctrine of the Power of the Keys; somewhat to open the words of the Text, whereon that power is built. Five words require a little clearing.

1. What is here meant by the Kingdom of Heaven?

2. What are the Keys of this Kingdom, and giving of them?

3. What are the acts of these Keys, which are said to be binding and loosing?

4. What is the object of these acts to be bound or loosed here put under a general name: *Whatsoever*?

5. Who is the subject recipient of this power, or to whom is this power given? *To thee will I give the Keys etc.*

1. For the first: By the Kingdom of Heaven is here meant, both the Kingdom of Grace, which is the Church; and the Kingdom of Glory, which is the highest heavens: For Christ giving to *Peter* the Keys of the Kingdom of Heaven, conveys therewith not only this Power to bind on earth (that is, in the church on earth; for he gave him no power at all to bind in the world; The Kingdom of Christ is not of this world): but he gives him also this privilege: That what he bound on earth, should be bound in heaven. And heaven being distinguished from the Church on earth must needs be meant the Kingdom of Glory.

2. For the second: What the Keys of the Kingdom of Heaven be?

The Keys of the Kingdom are the Ordinances which Christ has instituted to be administered in his Church; as the preaching of the Word, (which is the opening and applying of it) also the administration of the Seals and Censures: For by the opening and applying of these, both the gates of the church here, and of heaven hereafter, are opened or shut to the sons of men.

And the giving of these Keys, implies, that Christ invests those to whom he gives them, with a power to open, and shut the gates of both. And this power lies, partly in their spiritual calling (whether it be their Office, or their Place and Order in the Church): and partly in the concourse and cooperation of the Spirit of Christ, accompanying the right dispensation of these Keys: that is of these Ordinances according to his will.

Moreover, these Keys are neither Sword nor Sceptre: No Sword, for they convey not civil power of bodily life and death; nor Sceptre, for they convey not Sovereign or Legislative power over the Church, but stewardly and ministerial. As the key of the house of David was given to Hilkiah (Isaiah 22:22) who succeeded Shebna in his office: and his office was, עַל־הַבָּיִת, over the house, *verse* 15 and the same word over the house, is translated Steward in the house, (Genesis 43:19).

3. Touching the third thing. What are the acts of these Keys?

The acts of these Keys are said here to be binding and loosing, which are not proper acts of material Keys; for their acts be opening and shutting, which argues the keys here spoken of be not material keys, but metaphorical; and yet being keys, they have a power also of opening and shutting: For Christ, who has the sovereign power of these Keys, he is said to have the key of *David,* to open, and no man to shut; to shut, and no man to open (Revelation 3:7), which implies, that these Keys of Christ's Kingdom have such a power of opening and shutting, as that they do thereby bind and loose, retain and remit; in opening, they loose, and remit; in shutting they bind, and retain; which will more appear in opening the fourth point.

4. The fourth point then is: What is the subject to be bound and loosed? The Test in Matthew 16:9, faith, *whatsoever,* which reach's not (so far as the Papists would stretch it) to whatsoever oaths, or covenants, or contracts, or counsels, or laws; as if whatsoever oaths of allegiance, covenants of lease or marriage, etc. the Pope ratifies or dissolves on earth, should be ratified or dissolved in heaven: No, this is not the Key of the Kingdom of Heaven, but the key of the bottomless pit (Revelation 9:1). But this word, *whatsoever,* is here put in the Neuter Gender, (not in the Masculine, *whomsoever*) to imply both things and persons: Things, as sins, persons as those that commit them. For so, our Saviour speaks of the same acts of the same Keys (John 20:21), he explains himself thus: *Whose sins forever ye remit, they are remitted, and whose sins soever ye retain, they are retained.* Whatsoever you bind on earth is as much therefore, as whose sins soever you retain on earth; and whatsoever you loose on earth, is as much as whose sins soever you loose on earth.

Now, this binding and loosing of whatsoever sins, in whosoever commit them, is partly in the conscience of the sinner, and partly in his outward estate in the Church, which is wont to be expressed in other terms, either *in foro interiori,* or *in foro exteriori* (1): As when in the dispensation of the Ordinances of God, a sinner is convinced to lie under the guilt of sin, then his sin is retained, his conscience is bound under the guilt of it, and himself bound under some Church censure, according to the quality and desert of his offence; and if his sin be the more heinous, himself is shut out from the communion of the Church: But when a sinner repents of his sin, and confesses it before the Lord, and (if it be known) before his people also, and then in the ministry of the Doctrine and Discipline of the gospel, his sin is remitted, and his conscience loosed from the guilt of it, and himself has open and free entrance, both unto the promise of the gospel, and into the gates of the holy communion of the Church.

5. The fifth point to be explained, is, to whom is this power of the keys given?

The Text says, to thee *Simon Peter,* the son of *Jona,* whom Christ blesses, and pronounces blessed upon his holy confession of Christ, the Son of the living God, and upon the same occasion promises both to use Him and his confession, as an instrument to the lay the foundation of his Church; and also to give him the keys of his Church, for the well ordering and governing of it. But it has proved a busy Question. How *Peter* is to be considered in receiving this power of the keys, whether as an Apostle, or as an Elder, (for an Elder also he was 1 Peter 5:1) or as a Believer professing his faith before the Lord Jesus, and his fellow Brethren. Now because we are as well studious of peace, as of truth, we will not lean to one of these interpretations, more than to another. Take any of them; it will not hinder our purpose in this ensuing discourse, though (to speak ingenuously and without offence what we conceive) the sense of the words will be most full, if all the several considerations were taken jointly together. Take *Peter,* considered not only as an Apostle, but an Elder also, yea, and a Believer too; professing his faith, all may well stand together. For there is a different power given to all these, to an Apostle, to an Elder, to a Believer, and *Peter*, was all these, and received all the power which was given by Christ to any of these, or to all of these together. For as the Father sent Christ, so Christ sent *Peter* (as well as any Apostle) *cum amplitudine, & plenitudine potestatis* **(2)**, (so far as either any Church Officer, or the whole Church itself, was capable of it) (John 20:21). So that *Austin*, did not mistake, when he said *Peter* received the keys in the name of the Church. Nevertheless, we from this place in (Matthew 16:19) will challenge no further power, either to the Presbytery, or to the Fraternity of the Church, than is more expressly granted to them in other Scriptures. Now in other Scriptures it appears: First, that Christ gave the Power of retaining or remitting of sins (that is, the power of binding and loosing, the whole power of the keys) to all the Apostles as well as to *Peter,* (John 20:21, 23). Secondly, it appears also, that the Apostles commanded the rule and government of every particular church to the Elders (the Presbytery) of that church (Hebrews 13:17; 1 Timothy 5:17). And therefore Christ gave the power of the keys to them also. Thirdly, it appears further, that Christ gave the power of the keys to the Body likewise of the Church, even to the Fraternities with the Presbytery. For the Lord Jesus communicates the power of binding and loosing to the Apostles, or Elders, together with the whole Church, when they are met in his Name, and agree together in the censure of an offender (Matthew 18:17-18). If an offender (says he) *neglect to hear the Church, let him be to thee as an Heathen or a Publican,* that is let him be excommunicated. Which censure administered by them, with the whole Church, he ratifies with the promise of the power of the Keys: *Verily I say unto you, whatsoever you shall bind on earth, shall be bound in heaven, and whatsoever you shall loose on earth, shall be loosed in heaven.* In which place, howsoever there be some difference between Classical and Congregational Divines, what should be meant by the *Church (Tell the Church)* whether the Presbytery or the Congregation; yet all agree in this, (and it is agreement in the truth, which we seek for). That no offender is to be excommunicated but with some concurse of the Congregation, at least by way: 1. Of consent of the sentence. 2. Of actual execution of it, by withdrawing themselves from the offender so convicted and censured. Now this consent and concurse of the Congregation, which is requisite to the power and validity of the censure, we conceive is some part of the exercise of the power of the Keys.

So that when Christ said to *Peter, To thee will I give the Keys of the kingdom of heaven:* If *Peter* then received the whole power of the Keys, then he stood in the room and name of all such, as have received any part of the power of the Keys, whether Apostles or Elders, or Churches. Or, if he stood in the room of an Apostle only, yet that hinders not, but that as he there received the power of an Apostle, so the rest of the Apostles received the same power, either there, or elsewhere: and the Presbytery of each Church received, if not there, yet elsewhere, the power belongs to their office: and in like sort each Church or

Congregation of professed Believers, received that portion also of Church power which belonged to them.

CHAPTER 2

Of the Distribution of the Keys, and their power, or of the several sorts thereof.

THE ordinary Distribution of the Keys, is wont to be thus delivered. There is *clavis* (1. *Scientiae,*   A Key of knowledge, and a

(2. *Potestatis, Key* of power: and the Key of power is (1. *Ordinis,* Either a Key of Order, or a Key of (2. *Jurisdictionis, Jurisdiction.*

This distribution though it goes for current both amongst Protestant and Papists; yet we crave leave to express, what in it does not fully satisfy us. Four things in it seem defective to us:

1. That the Key of the Kingdom of heaven should be left without power: For here in this distribution, the key of knowledge is contradistinguished from a Key of power.

2. There is a real defect in omitting an integral part of the keys, which is the key of Church liberty. But no marvel, though the Popish Clergy omitted it, who have oppressed all Church liberty: and Protestant Churches, having recovered the liberty of preaching the gospel, and Ministry of the Sacraments, some of them have looked no further, nor so much as discerned their defect of Church liberty in point of Discipline: and others finding themselves wronged in withholding a key or power, which belongs to them, have wrested to themselves an undue power, which belongs not to them, the key of Authority.

3. There is another defect in the Distribution, in the dividing the key of Order from the key of Jurisdiction; of purpose to make way, for the power of Chancellors and Commissionaires *in foro exteriori*: who though they want the key of Order, (having never entered into holy orders, as they are called, or at most into the order of Deacons only, whereof our Lord spoke nothing touching Jurisdiction) yet they have been invested with Jurisdiction, yes, and more than ministerial authority, even above

those Elders, who labour in word and doctrine: By this sacrilegious breach of order (which has been, as it were, the breaking of the Files and Ranks in an Army, Satan has routed and ruined a great part of the liberty and purity of Churches, and all the Ordinances of Christ in them.

4. A fourth defect (but yet the least, which we observe in this Distribution) is, that order is appropriated to the Officers of the Church only. For though we be far from allowing that sacrilegious usurpation of the Ministers Office, which we hear of (to our grief) to be practised in some places, that private Christians ordinarily take upon them to preach the gospel publicly, and to minister Sacraments: yet we put a difference between Office and Order. Office, we look at as peculiar to those, who are (set apart for some peculiar Function in the Church, who are either Elders or Deacons. But Order (speaking of Church order properly taken) is common to all the members of the Church, whether Officers or private Brethren. There is an order as well in them that are subject, as in them that rule. There is a τάξι as well τών ύποτακων, as των έπιτακικων. The maid in Athens is said, θεράπαινη ταξίν έπιλάβουσα as well as her Mistress. Yet if any were willing to make office and order equipollent, we will not contend about words, so there be no erroneous apprehension wrapt into the matter.

To come therefore to such a Distribution of the Keys as is more suitable to Scripture phrase. For it becomes true *Israelites*, rather to speak the language of *Canaan,* than the language of *Ashdod.*

When *Paul* beheld, and rejoiced to behold, how the Church of *Colosse* had received the Lord Jesus, and walked in him; he sums up all their Church estate, *to know,* their beauty and power, in these two, Faith and Order, (Colossians 2:5-6).

There is therefore a Key of Faith, and a Key of Order.

The Key of Faith is the same, which the Lord Jesus calls the Key of knowledge, (Luke 11:52) and which he complains, the lawyers had taken away. Now that key of knowledge Christ speaks of, was such, that if it had not been taken away, they that had it, had power by it to enter into the kingdom of heaven themselves, and it may be, to open the door to others, to enter also. Now such a knowledge, whereby a man has power to enter into heaven is only Faith, which is often therefore called Knowledge, as (Isaiah 53:11) *By the knowledge of him shall my righteous servant justify many*: that is, by faith in Christ. And (John 17:3) *this is eternal life to know thee:* that is, to believe on thee. This Key, therefore, the key of knowledge, (saving knowledge) or, which is all one, the Key of Faith, is common to all believers. A faithful soul knowing the Scriptures and Christ in them, receives Christ, and enters through him into the kingdom of heaven, both here, and hereafter. Here he enters into a state of grace through faith: and by the profession of his faith, he enters also into the fellowship of the Church (which is the kingdom of heaven upon earth): and by the same faith, as he believes to justification, so he makes confession to salvation, which is perfected in the kingdom of glory, (Romans 10:10).

The Key of Order is the power whereby every member of the Church walks orderly himself, according to his place in the Church, and helps his brethren to walk orderly also.

It was that which the Apostles and Elders called upon *Paul*, so to carry himself before the *Jews* in the Temple, that he might make it appear to all men that he walked orderly (Acts 21:18, 24). Orderly, to know, according to the orders of the Jewish Church, with whom he then conversed. And it was the commandment, which *Paul* gave to the whole Church of Thessalonica, and to all the members of it, to *withdraw themselves from every brother that walketh disorderly* (2 Thessalonians 3:6). Their withdrawing from him that walked disorderly was the exercise of their key of order. And it was a like exercise of the same key of order, when he requires the Brethren to warn the *unruly,* which is, (in the original) the same word, to admonish the *disorderly* (1 Thessalonians 5:14). And this key of order (to know, order understood in this sense) is common to all the members of the church, whether Elders or brethren.

Furthermore, of *Order* there are *two keys*: a key of *power,* or *interest*: And the key of *Authority* or *Rule*. The first of these is termed in the Scriptures, *Liberty*: So distinguishing it from that part of *Rule* and *Authority* in the Officers of the Church. We speak not here of that spiritual liberty, whether of *impunity,* whereby the children of God are

29

set free by the blood of Christ from Satan, hell, bondage of sin, curse of the Moral Law, and service of the Ceremonial Law: nor of *immunity* whereby we have *power to be called the sons of God,* to come boldly unto the throne of grace in prayer, and as heirs of glory, to look for our inheritance in light: but of that *external liberty,* or *interest* which Christ also has purchased for his people, as liberty to enter into the fellowship of his Church, liberty to choose and all well gifted men to office in that his Church: liberty to partake in Sacraments, or Seals of the Covenant of the Church, liberty and interest to join with officers in due censure of offenders, and the like. This liberty and the acts of it are often exemplified in the Acts of the Apostles: and the Apostle *Paul* called it expressly by the name of liberty. *Brethren* (says he) *you have been called unto LIBERTY, only use not your liberty as an occasion to the flesh, but by love serve one another* (Galatians 5:13). That the Apostle by that liberty means Church-liberty, or power in ordering Church-affairs, will evidently appear, if we consult with the context, rather than with Commentators. For the Apostle having spent the former part of the Epistle, partly in the confirmation of his calling, partly in disputation against justification by the works of the law, to the end of *verse* 8 of Chapter 5. In the ninth verse he descends not to exhort unto *bonos mores* (good conduct), in general, (as usually Commentators take it) but to instruct in Church Discipline, in which he gives three or four directions to the tenth *verse* of Chapter 6.

1. Touching the censure of those corrupt teachers, who had perverted and troubled them with that corrupt Doctrine of justification by works *Chapter* 5 *verse* 9 to the end of the Chapter.

2. Touching the gentle admonition and restoring of a brother fallen by infirmity *Chapter* 6 *verses* 1 *to* 5.

3. Touching the maintenance of their Ministers, *verses* 6-8 and beneficence to others, *verses* 9-10.

Touching the first, the censure of their corrupt Teachers. (1). He lays for the ground of it (that which himself gave for the ground of the excommunication of the incestuous Corinth, 1 Corinthians 5:6) *A little leaven leaveneth the whole lump* (Galatians 5:9). (2). He presumes the

Church will be of the same mind with him and concur in the censure of him that troubled them with corrupt doctrine *verse* 10; (from fellowship with corrupt doctrine he clears himself, *verse* 11). (3). He proceeds to declare, what censure he wishes might be dispensed against him, and the rest of those corrupt Teachers, *I would* (says he) *they were even cut off that trouble you*: cut off, to wit, by excommunication, *verse* 12. Now lest it should be objected by the brethren of the Church: But what power have we to cut them off? The Apostle answers, they have a power and liberty (to know, to join with the founder part of the *Presbytery*, in casting them out, or cutting them off): *For brethren* (says he) *you are called unto liberty.* If it should be further objected, yes, but give the people this power and liberty in some cases, either to cast off their Teachers, or to cut them off, the people will soon take advantage to abuse this liberty unto much carnal licentiousness. The Apostle prevents that with a word of wholesome counsel: *Brethren* (says he) *you have been called unto liberty: only use not your liberty as an occasion to the flesh, but by love serve one another, verse* 13, and thereupon seasonably purifies this counsel with a caveat (warning) to beware of abusing this liberty to carnal contention, (an usual disease of popular liberty) and withal dehorts them from all other fruits of the flesh, to the end of the Chapter.

Evident therefore it is, that there is a key of power or liberty given to the Church (to the Brethren with the Elders) as to open a door of entrance to the Ministers calling; so to shut the door of entrance against them in some cases, as when through corrupt and pernicious doctrine, they turn from Shepherds to become ravenous Wolves. Having spoken then of that first key of order, namely, the key of *power*, (in a more large sense) or liberty in the *Church*, there remains the other *key of order*, which is the key of *Authority* or of *Rule*, in a more strict sense, which is in the *Elders* of the Church.

Authority is a moral power, in a superior order, (or state) *binding and releasing an inferior in point of subjection.*

This key when it was promised to *Peter* (Matthew 16:19) and given to him with the rest of the Apostles (John 20:23) they thereby had power to bind and loose: and it is the same Authority which is given to their

31

successors the Elders, whereby they are called to feed and rule the Church of God, as the Apostles had done before them (Acts 20:28). And indeed by opening and applying the Law (the spirit of bondage accompanying the same) they bind sinners under the curse, and their consciences under guilt of sin, and fear of wrath, and shut the kingdom of heaven against them. And by opening and applying the gospel (the Spirit of Adoption accompanying the same) they remit sin and loose the consciences of believing repenting souls from guilt of sin, and open to them the doors of heaven. By virtue of this key, as they preach *with all authority*, not only the doctrine of the law, but also the Covenant of the Gospel; so they administer the seals of it, Baptism, and the Lords Supper. By virtue of this key they with the Church do bind an obstinate offender under excommunication (Matthew 18:17-18), and release, and forgive him upon his repentance (2 Corinthians 2:7).

This Distribution of the *keys*, and so of *Spiritual power*, in the things of Christ's kingdom, we have received from the Scripture. But if any men out of love to Antiquity, do rather affect to keep to the terms of the former more ancient Distribution (as there be who are as loath to change *Antiquos terminos verborum,* as *agrorum*) **(3)** we would not stick upon the words rightly explained, out of desire both to judge and speak the same things with fellow brethren. Only then let them allow some spiritual power to the key of knowledge, though not Church power. And in Church power let them put in as well a *key of liberty*, that is, a power of privilege *of interest*, as a *key of Authority*. And by their key of order, as they do understand the key of office, so let them not divide from it the key of jurisdiction (for Christ has given no jurisdiction, but to whom he has given office) and so we willingly consent with them.

CHAPTER 3

Of the Subject of the power of the keys, to whom they are committed: and the first of the key of Knowledge, and Order.

AS the keys of the kingdom of heaven be diverse, so are the subjects to who they are committed, diverse: as in the natural body, diversity of functions belongs to diversity of members.

1. The *key of knowledge* (or which is all one, the key of Faith) belongs to the faithful, whether joined to any particular Church or not. As in the primitive times, men of grown years were first called and converted to the faith, before they were received into the Church: And even now an Indian or Pagan may not be received into the Church, till he have first received the faith, and have made profession of it before the Lord, and the Church: which argues, that the key of knowledge is given not only to the Church, but to some before they enter into the Church. And yet to Christians for the Churches sake: that they who receive this grace of faith, by it may receive Christ and his benefits, and therewith may receive also this privilege, to find an *open door* set before them, to enter into the fellowship of the Church.

2. The *key of order* (speaking as we do of Church order, as *Paul* does Colossians 2:5) belongs to all such, who are in Church order, whether *Elders* or *Brethren*. For though Elders be in superior order, by reason of their office, yet the brethren (over whom the Elders are made Overseers and Rulers) they stand also in order, even in orderly subjection, according to the order of the Gospel. It is true, every faithful soul that has received a key of knowledge, is bound to watch over his neighbours soul, as his own, and to admonish him of his sin, unless he be a scorner: but this he does, *Non ratione ordinis, sed intuitu charitatis*: not by virtue of a state of order which he is in (till in Church fellowship) but as common Christian love and charity. But every faithful Christian who stands in Church order is bound to do the same, as well *respectu ordinis,* as *intuitu charitatis,* by virtue of that royal Law, not only of love, but of Church order (Matthew

18:15-17), whereby if his brother who offended him, does not listen to his conviction and admonition, he is then according to order, to proceed further, taking one or two with him: and if the offender refuse to hear them also then he is by order to tell the Church, and afterwards walk towards him, as God shall direct the Church to order it.

Chapter 4

Of the subject to whom the Key of Church privilege, power, or Liberty is given.

THIS key is given to the Brethren of the Churches for so says the Apostle in (Galatians 5:13), (in the place quoted and opened before) *Brethren, you have been called to liberty.*

And indeed, as it is the εύ ειναι εὐεξία and εὐπραξία, , of a Commonwealth, the right and due establishment and balancing of the *liberties* or *privileges* of the people (which is in a true sense, may be called a *power*) and the *authority* of the Magistrates so it is the safety of Church estate, the right and due settling and ordering of the holy *power* of the *privileges* and *liberties* of the Brethren, and the ministerial authority of the Elders. The gospel allows no Church authority (or rule properly so called) to the Brethren, but reserves that wholly to the Elders; and yet prevents the tyranny and oligarchy, and exorbitancy of the Elders, by the large and firm establishment of the liberties of the brethren, which arises to a *power* in them. *Bucers* axiom is here notable; *Potestas penes omnem Ecclesiam est; Authoritas ministerii penes Presbyteros et Episcopos* **(4)**. In Matthew 16:19 where *Potestas,* or power being contradistinguished from *Authoritas, Authority* is nothing else but a liberty or privilege.

The liberties of the Brethren, or the Church consisting of them, are many and great.

1. The Church of Brethren has the *power, privileges,* and *liberty* to choose their Officers. In the choice of an Apostle into the place of *Judas,* the people went as far as humane vote and suffrage could go. Out of 120 persons (*verse* 15) they chose out, and presented two, out of which two (because an Apostle was to be designed immediately by God) God by lot chose one; And yet this one so chosen of God, Συγκατεψηφίσθη, *communibus omnium saffragiis inter duodecim Apostolos allectus est,* (*verse* 26) **(5)**, was counted amongst the Apostles by common suffrages

of them all. And this place *Cyprian* presses amongst others, to confirm the *power* (that is ἐξουσιαν, or *privilege*, or *liberty*) of the people, in choosing or refusing their ministers. *Plebi Christiana* (says he) *vel maxime potestatem habet, vel dignos Sacredotes eligendi, vel indignos recusandi*, Epistle. 4. Lib. 1. **(6)**.

The like, or greater liberty is generally approved by the best of our Divines (studious of Reformation) from (Acts 14:23). They *ordained them Elders, chosen by lifting up of hands.*

The same *power* is clearly expressed in the choice of Deacons, (Acts 6:3, 5-6). The Apostles did not choose the Deacons, but called the multitude together, and said unto them, *Brethren, look you out seven men amongst you, whom we may appoint over this business: And the saying pleased the whole multitude, and they chose* Stephen, etc.

2. It is a *privilege,* or a *liberty* the Church has received, to send forth one or more of their Elders, as the public service of Christ and of the Church may require. Thus *Epiphroditus* was a *Messenger* or *Apostle* of the Church of *Philippi* unto *Paul*, (Philippians 2:25).

3. The *Brethren* of the Church have *power* and *liberty* of propounding any just exception against such as offer themselves to be admitted unto their communion, or unto the seals of it: Hence *Saul*, when he offered himself to the communion of the Church at *Jerusalem*, was not at first admitted thereto, upon an exception taken against him by the *Disciples*, till that exception was removed (Acts 9:26-27) and *Peter* did not admit the family of *Cornelius* to Baptism, till he had inquired of the *Brethren*, if any of them had any exception against it, (Acts 10:47).

4. As the *Brethren* have a *power* of order, and the *privilege* to expostulate with their *Brethren,* in case of private scandals, according to the rule (Matthew 18:15-16). So in case of public scandal, the whole Church of *Brethren* have *power* and *privilege* to join with the *Elders,* in inquiring, hearing, judging of public scandals; so as to bind notorious offenders and impenitents under censure, and to forgive the repentant: For when Christ commands a brother, in case that offence cannot be healed privately, then to *tell the Church,* (Matthew 18:17) it necessarily

implies that the Church must hear him, and inquire into the offence complained of, and judge of the offence as they find it upon inquiry.

When the *Brethren* that were of the circumcision expostulated with *Peter* about his communion with *Cornelius,* and his uncircumcised family, *Peter* did not reject them, and their complaint against him, as transgressing the bounds of their just *power* and *privilege,* but readily addressed himself to give satisfaction to them all (Acts 11:2-18). The *Brethren of the Church of Corinth* being gathered together with their Elders, *in the name of the Lord Jesus,* and with *his power, did deliver the incestuous person to Satan* (1 Corinthians 5:4-5). And Paul *reproved* them all, Brethren as well as Elders, that they had no sooner put him away from amongst them *verse* 2, and expressly he allowed to them all power *to judge* them that are within *verse* 22. Yes, and from here argues, in all the Saints, even in the meanest of the Saints, an ability to judge between brethren, in the things of this life, as those that have received such a Spirit of discerning from Christ, by which they shall one day judge the world, even Angels, so in the next Chapter the 6th of that 1 Corinthians 1-5. And the same *Brethren* of the same Church, as well as *Elders,* he increases *to forgive* the same incestuous *Corinthian,* upon his repentance (2 Corinthians 2:7-8).

If it be said, to *judge* is an act of rule; and to be Rulers of the Church, is not given to all the Brethren, but to the Elders only:

Answer. All judgement is not an act of authority or rule; for there is a judgement of discretion, by way of *privilege*, as well as of authority by way of sentence: That of discretion is common to all the *Brethren,* as well as that of authority belongs to the *Presbytery* of that Church. In *England,* the Jury by their verdict, as well as the Judge by his sentence, do both of them judge the same criminal; yet in the Jury their verdict is but an act of their popular liberty: In the Judge it is an act of his judicial authority.

If it were demanded, what difference is there between these two?

The answer is ready, Great is the difference: for though the Jury have given up their judgement and verdict, yet the criminal is not thereupon legally condemned, much less executed, but upon the sentence of the

Judge: In like sort here, though the brethren of the Church do with one accord give their vote and judgement for the censure of an offender, yet he is not thereby censured, till upon the sentence of the Presbytery. If it was said again; yes, but it is an act of authority to bind and loose, and the power to bind and loose, Christ gave to the whole Church (Matthew 18:18).

Answer. The whole Church may be said to bind and loose, in that the Brethren consent, and concur with the Elders, both before the Censure in discerning it to be just and equal, and in declaring their discernment, by lifting up of their hands, or by silence: and after the censure, in rejecting the offender censured from their wanted Communion. And yet their discerning or approving of the justice of the censure beforehand is not preventing of the Elders in their work. For the Elders before that have not only privately examined the offender and his offence, and the proofs of it, to prepare the matter and ripen it for the Churches cognisance: but do also publicly revise the heads of all the material passages of it before the Church: and do with all declare to the Church the counsel and will of God therein, that they may rightly discern and approve what censure the Lord requires to be administered in such a case. So that the peoples discerning and approving the justice of the censure before it be administered, arises from the Elders former instruction and direction of them therein: Whereunto the people give consent, in obedience to the will and rule of Christ. Hence is that speech of the Apostle; *we have in readiness to revenge all disobedience, when your OBEDIENCE IS FULFILLED,* (2 Corinthians 10:6). The Apostles revenge of disobedience by way of reproof in preaching, does not follow the people's obedience, but proceeds whether the people obey it or not. It was therefore their revenge of disobedience by way of censure in discipline, which they had in readiness, when the obedience of the Church is fulfilled in discerning and approving the Equity of the Censure, which the Apostles or Elders have declared to them from the Word.

This power or privilege of the Church in dealing in this sort with a scandalous offender, may not be limited only to a private brother offending, but may reach also to an offensive Elder. For (as has been touched already) it is plain that the Brethren of the Circumcision, supposing *Peter* to have given an offence in eating with men uncircumcised, they openly expostulated with about his offence: and he stood not with them upon terms of his Apostleship, much less of his Eldership, but willingly submitted himself to give satisfaction to them all (Acts 11:2-18). And *Paul* writes to the Church of *Colosse,* to deal with *Archippus,* warning him to see to the fulfilling of his Ministry (Colossians 4:17). And very pregnant is his direction to the *Galatians,* for their proceeding to the utmost with their corrupt and scandalous false Teachers. *I would* (says he) *they were even cut off that trouble you;* and that upon this very ground of their *liberty,* (Galatians 5:12-13) as has been opened above in *Chapter 2.*

But whether the Church has power or liberty for proceeding to the utmost censure of their whole Presbytery is a Question of more difficulty.

For 1. It cannot well be conceived that the whole Presbytery should be proceeded against, but that by reason of their strong influence into the hearts of many of the Brethren, a strong party of the Brethren will be ready to side with them: and in case of finding dissension and opposition, the Church ought not to proceed without consulting the Synod. As when there arose dissension in the Church at *Antioch,* and SIDING, (or as the word is στάσις) they sent up to the Apostles and Elders at *Jerusalem,* who in way of Synod determined the business (Acts 15:2-23). A precedent and pattern of due Church proceedings in case of dissension, when some take with one side, some with another. But of that more hereafter.

2. *Excommunication* is one of the *highest* acts of *Rule* in the Church, and therefore cannot be performed but by some Rulers. Now where all the Elders are culpable, there be no Rulers left in that Church to censure them. As therefore the presbytery cannot excommunicate the whole Church, (though Apostate) for they must tell the Church, and join with the Church in that Censure: so neither can the Church excommunicate the whole *Presbytery,* because they have not received from Christ an office of rule, without their Officers.

If it be said, the *twenty four Elders* (who represent the private members of the Church, as the *four living Creatures* do the four Officers) had all of them *Crowns* upon their heads, and *sat* upon *thrones* (Revelation 4:4), which are signs of regal authority: The answer is, the crowns and thrones argue them to be *Kings,* no more than their *white raiment's* argue them to be *Priests, verse* 4, but neither Priests nor Kings by Office, but by liberty to perform like spiritual duties by grace, which the other do by grace and office: As Priests they offer up spiritual sacrifices; and as Kings they rule their lusts, passions, themselves, and their families, yes, the world and Church also after a sort: the world, by improving it to spiritual advantage: and the Church, by appointing their own Officers, and likewise in censuring their offenders, not only by their officers, (which is as much as Kings are not wont to do), but also by their own royal assent, which Kings are not wont to do, but only in the execution of Nobles.

But nevertheless, though the Church want authority to excommunicate their Presbytery, yet they want not liberty to withdraw from them: or so *Paul* instructs and beseeches the Church of *Rome* (whom the holy Ghost foresaw would most stand in need of this counsel) to make use of this liberty: *I beseech you* (says he) *mark such as cause divisions and offences, contrary to the DOCTRINE you have received,* καὶ ἐκκλίνατε ἀπ αὐτων, *WITHDRAW from them.*

So then, by the agitation of this objection, there appear two liberties of the Church more to be added to the former.

One is this (which is the fifth liberty in members) the Church has liberty in case of dissension amongst themselves to resort to a Synod (Acts 15:1-2). Where also it appears the *Brethren* enjoyed this liberty, to dispute their doubts till they were satisfied, *verses 7 and* 12, to join with the *Apostles* and *Elders* in the definitive sentence, and in the promulgation of the same, *verses* 22 *and* 23.

The sixth Liberty of the Church is. To withdraw from the communion of those, whom they want authority to excommunicate. For as they set up the Presbytery, by professing their subjection to them in the Lord: so they avoid them by professed withdrawing their subjection from them according to God.

A seventh and last Liberty of the Church, is Liberty of communion with other churches. Communion we say; for it is a great Liberty, that no particular church stands in subjection to another particular church, no not to a Cathedral Church; but that all the Churches enjoy mutual brotherly communion amongst themselves; which communion is mutually exercised amongst them seven ways, which for brevity and memory sake, we sum up in seven words. 1. By way of *Participation*. 2. Of *Recommendation*. 3. Of *Consultation*. 4. Of *Congregation* into a Synod. 5. Of *Contribution*. 6. Of *Admonition*. 7. Of *Propagation* or *Multiplication* of Churches.

1. By way of *Participation*; the members of one church occasionally coming to another church, where the Lords Supper comes to be administered, are willingly admitted to partake with them at the Lords Supper, in case that neither themselves, nor the churches from whence they came, do lie under any public offence. For we receive the Lords Supper, not only as a Seal of our communion with the Lord Jesus, and with his members in our own Church, but also in all the churches of the Saints.

2. By way of *Recommendation*; Letters are sent from one church to another, recommending to their watchfulness and communion, any of their members, who by occasion of business, are for a time to reside amongst them. As *Paul* sent Letters of *Recommendation* to the Church of *Rome,* on behalf of Phebe, a Deaconess of the Church of *Cenchrea,* (Romans 16:1-2). And of these kinds of Letters he speaks to the Church of *Corinth* also though not as needful to himself (who was well known to them) yet for others (2 Corinthians 3:1).

But if a member of one church have just occasion to remove himself and his family, to take up his settled habitation in another church, then the Letters written by the church in his behalf, do recommend him to their perpetual watchfulness and communion. And if the other church have no just cause to refuse him, they of his own church do by those letters wholly dismiss him from themselves; whereupon the letters (for distinction sake) are called letters of dismission; which indeed do not differ from the other, but in the durance of the recommendation, the one recommending him for a time, the other for ever.

3. By way of *Consultation*, one church has liberty of communicating with another to require their judgement and counsel, touching any person or cause, wherewith they may be better acquainted then themselves. Thus the Church of *Antioch,* by their messengers, consulted with the Church at *Jerusalem*, touching the necessity of circumcision (Acts 15:3), although the consultation brought forth a further effect of communion with churches; that is to say, their Congregation into a Synod. Which is the fourth way of communion of churches: All of the churches have the like liberty of sending their messengers to debate the determine in a Synod, such matters as do concern them all; As the Church of *Antioch* sent messengers to *Jerusalem* for resolution and satisfaction in a doubt that troubled them: the like liberty by proportion might any other church have taken; yes many churches together; yes all the churches in the world, in any case that might concern them all. What authority these Synods have received, and may put forth, will come to be considered in the sequel.

A fifth way of communion of churches is the Liberty of giving and receiving mutual supplies and assistance one from another. The Church at *Jerusalem* communicated to the churches of the *Gentiles*, their spiritual treasures of gifts of Grace; and the churches of the *Gentiles* ministered back again to them, liberal oblations of outward beneficence, (Romans 15:26-27; Acts 11:29-30). When the church of *Antioch* abounded with more variety of spiritual gifted men, then the state of their own church stood in need of; they fasted and prayed; as for other ends, so for the enlargement of Christ's Kingdom in improvement of them. And the Holy Ghost opened them a door for the assistance of many countries about them, by the sending forth of some of them (Acts 13:1-3).

A sixth way of communion of churches is by way of mutual admonition, when a public offence is found amongst any of them: For as *Paul* had liberty to admonish *Peter* before the whole church at *Antioch*, when he saw him walk not with a right foot, (and yet *Paul* had no authority over *Peter*, but only had equal mutual interest one in another, Galatians 2:11-14). So by the same proportion, one Church has liberty to admonish another, though they are both of them of equal authority; seeing one

Church has as much interest in another, as one Apostle in another. And if by the royal law of love, one Brother has liberty to admonish his Brother in the same Church (Matthew 18:15-16), then by the same rule of brotherly love, and mutual watchfulness, one Church has power to admonish another, in faithfulness to the Lord, and unto them. The Church in the *Canticles (Song of Solomon)* took care not only for her own members, but for her little sister, which she thought had no breasts; yes and consulted with other Churches what to do for her, (Song of Solomon 8:8). And would she not then have taken like care, in case their little sister having breasts, her breasts had been distempered, and given corrupt matter instead of milk?

A seventh way of communion of Churches mat be by way of propagation and multiplication of Churches: As when a particular Church of Christ shall grow so full of members, as all of them cannot hear the voice of their Ministers; then as an Hive full of Bees swarms forth, so is the Church occasioned to send forth a sufficient number of her members, fit to enter into a Church-state, and to carry along Church-work amongst themselves. And for that end they either send forth some one or other of their Elders with them, to direct them where to procure such to come unto them. The like course is wont to be taken, when sundry Christians coming over from one country to another; such as are come over first, and are themselves full of company, direct those that come after them, and assist them in like sort, in the combination of themselves into Church-order, according to the Rule of the Gospel. Though the Apostles are dead, whose office it was to plant, and gather, and multiply Churches; yet the work is not dead, but the same power of the keys is left with the Churches in common, and with each particular Church for her part, according to their measure, to propagate and enlarge the Kingdom of Christ (as God shall give opportunity) throughout all generations.

Chapter 5

Of the Subject to whom the Key of Authority is committed.

THE key of *Authority* or *Rule*, is committed to the Elders of the Church, and so the act of Rule is made the proper act of their office, *The Elders that rule well, etc,* (1 Timothy 5:17; Hebrews 13:7, 17).

The special acts of this rule are many.

The first and principal is that which the *Elders who labour in the Word and Doctrine,* are chiefly to attend unto, that is, the *preaching of the Word with all Authority,* and that, which is annexed thereto, the administration of the Sacraments, or Seals. *Speak, rebuke, and exhort* (says *Paul* to *Titus*) *with all authority* (Titus 2:15). And that the administration of the seals is annexed thereto is plain from (Matthew 28:19-20). *Go* (says Christ to the Apostles) *make Disciples, and baptize them, etc.*

If it were objected, private members may all of them prophesy publicly (1 Corinthians 14:31), and therefore also baptize: and so this act of authority is not peculiar to preaching Elders.

Answer. 1. The place in Corinth does not speak of ordinary private members, but of men furnished with extraordinary gifts. Kings at the time of their Coronation give many extraordinarily large gifts, which they do not daily pour out in like sort in their ordinary government. Christ soon after his ascension poured out a larger measure of his Spirit than in times succeeding. The members of the Church of Corinth (as of many others in those primitive times) were *enriched with all knowledge, and in all utterance* (1 Corinthians 1:5). And the same persons that had the *gift of prophecy* in the Church of Corinth had also *the gift of tongues*, which put upon the Apostle a necessity to take them off from their frequent speaking with Tongues, by preferring prophecy before it (1 Corinthians 14:2-24). So that though all they might prophesy (as having extraordinary gifts for it), yet the like liberty is not allowed to them that want the like gifts. In the *Church* of *Israel*, none besides the *Priests* and *Levites*, did ordinarily prophesy, either in the Temple, or in the Synagogues, unless they were either furnished with extraordinary gifts of prophecy, (as the Prophets of *Israel*) or were set apart, and trained up, to prepare for such a calling, *as the sons of the prophets.* When Amos *was* forbidden by the *high Priest* of *Bethel,* to prophesy at *Bethel, Amos* does not allege nor plead the liberty of any *Israelite* to prophesy in the holy Assembly's, but alleges only his extraordinary calling (Amos 7:14-15). It appears also that the *sons of the Prophets,* that is, men set apart and trained up to prepare for that calling, were allowed the like liberty (1 Samuel 19:20).

Answer. 2. But neither the sons of the Prophets, nor the Prophets themselves, were wont to offer sacrifices in Israel, (except *Samuel* and *Eliah* by special direction) nor did the extraordinary Prophets in Corinth take upon them to administer Sacraments.

If any reply, that if the Prophets in the Church at Corinth had been endued with extraordinary gifts of prophecy they had not been *subject* to the *judgement of the Prophets,* which these are directed to be (1 Corinthians 14:21).

Answer. It follows not, for the People of God were to examine all prophecies *by the Law and the Testimony*, and not to receive them but according to that rule (Psalm 8:20). Yes and *Paul* himself refers all his Doctrine *to the Law and the Prophets* (Acts 26:21). And the Bereans are commended for examining *Paul's* Doctrine according to the Scriptures (Acts 17:11-12).

2. A second act of Authority common to the Elders, is they have power, as any weighty occasion shall require, *to call the Church* together, as the *Apostles called the Church together* for the election of Deacons (Acts 6:2). And in like sort are the *Priests* of the Old Testament stirred up to call a solemn Assembly, to gather the Elders, and all the inhabitants of the land, to *sanctify a fast* (Joel 1:13-14).

3. It is an act of their power, to examine, if the Apostles, then any others (whether officers or members) before they were received of the Church (Revelation 2:2).

A fourth act of their rule is, the *Ordination of Officers* (whom the people have chosen) whether Elders or Deacons (1 Timothy 4:14; Acts 6:6).

5. It is an act of the *Key of Authority*, that the Elders *open the doors of Speech and Silence* in the Assembly. They were the *Rulers of the Synagogue,* who sent *Paul* and *Barnabas* to open their mouths in a *word of exhortation* (Acts 13:15), and it is the same power which calls men to speak to put men in silence when they speak amiss. And yet when the *Elders* themselves do lie under offence, or under suspicion of it, the brethren have liberty to require satisfaction in a model manner, concerning any public breach of rule, as has been mentioned above out of (Acts 11:2-3, etc).

6. It belongs to the *Elders* to *prepare matters beforehand,* which are to be transacted by themselves, or others, in the face of the Congregation, as the *Apostles* and *Elders* being met at the house of *James*, gave direction to *Paul* how to carry himself that he might prevent the offence of the Church, when he should appear before them (Acts 21:18). Hence when the offence of a brother is (according to the rule in Matthew 18:17) to be brought to the *Church*, they are beforehand to consider and enquire whether the offence be really given or not, whether duly proved, and orderly proceeded in by the brethren, according to rule, and not duly satisfied by the offender: lest themselves and the Church, be openly cumbered with unnecessary and tedious agitations: but that all things transacted before the Church, be carried along with most expedition and best edification. In which respect they have power to reject causal and disorderly complaints, as well as to propound and handle just complaints before the congregation.

7. In the handling of an offence before the Church, the Elders have authority both *Jus dicere,* and *Setentiam ferre* **(7)**; When the offence appears truly scandalous; the Elders have power from God to inform the Church, what the *Law* (or *Rule* and *Will*) of *Christ* is for the censure of such an offence: And when the Church discerns the same, and has no just

exception against it, but condescends thereto, it is a further act of the Elders power, to *give sentence* against the offender. Both these acts of power in the Ministers of the Gospel are foretold by (Ezekiel 44:23-24). *They shall teach my people the difference between holy and profane and cause them to discern between the unclean and the clean.* And in *controversy they shall stand in judgement, and they shall judge it according to my judgement, etc.*

8. The Elders have power *to dismiss the Church* with *a blessing* in the name of the Lord (Numbers 6:23-26; Hebrews 7:7).

9. The Elders have received power to *charge* any of the people in *private,* that none of them live either *inordinately* without a calling, or *idlely* in their calling, or *scandalously* in any sort (2 Thessalonians 3:6 and verses 8, 10, 11, 12). The Apostles command argues a power in the Elders to charge these duties upon the people effectually.

10. What power belongs to the Elders in a *Synod* is more fitly to be spoken to in the *Chapter of Synods.*

11. In case the Church should fall away to blasphemy against Christ, and obstinate rejection and perfection of the way of grace, and either no Synod to be hoped for, or no help by a Synod, the Elders have power to *withdraw* (or *separate*) the *Disciples* from them, and to carry away the Ordinances with them, and therewith sadly to denounce the just judgement of God against them (Acts 19:9; Exodus 33:7; Mark 6:11; Luke 10:11; Acts 13:46).

Objection. But if Elders have all this power to exercise all these acts of Rule, partly over the private members, partly over the whole Church, how are they then called the *servants of the Church?* (2 Corinthians 4:5).

Answer. The Elders to be both Servants and Rulers of the Church, may both of them stand well together. For their Rule is not lordly, as if they ruled of themselves, or for themselves, but stewardly and ministerial, as ruling the Church for Christ, and for the Church, even their spiritual everlasting good. A Queen may call her servants, her Mariners, to pilot and conduct her over the Sea to such a Haven; yet they being called by her to such an office, she must not rule them in steering their course, but must submit her self to be ruled by them, till they have brought her to her desired Haven. So is the case between the Church and her Elders.

Chapter 6

Of the Power and Authority given to Synods.

Synods we acknowledge, being rightly ordered, as an Ordinance of Christ. Of their Assembly we find three just causes in Scripture. 1. When a Church wanting light or peace at home, desires the counsel and help of other churches, few or more. Thus the *Church at Antioch*, being annoyed with corrupt teachers, who darkened the light of the truth, and bred no small dissension amongst them in the Church; they sent *Paul* and *Barnabas* and other *messengers* unto the *Apostles* and *Elders* at Jerusalem, for the establishment of Truth and Peace. In joining the *Elders* to the *Apostles* (and that doubtless by the advice of *Paul* and *Barnabas*) it argues that they sent not to the *Apostles* as extraordinary and infallible, and authenticall Oracles of God, (for then what need the advice and help of *Elders*?) but as wise and holy guides of the church, who might not only relieve them by some wise counsel, and holy order, but also set a precedent to succeeding ages, how errors and dissensions in churches might be removed and healed. And the course, which the Apostles and Elders took for clearing the matter, was not by publishing the counsel of God with Apostolic authority, from immediate revelation, but by searching out the truth in an ordinary way of free disputation (Acts 15:7), which is a fit course for imitation in after ages, as it was seasonable practice for then.

2. Just consequence from Scripture gives us another ground for the assembly of many churches, or of their messengers, into a Synod, when any church lies under scandal, through corruption in doctrine and practice, and will not be healed by more private advertisements of their own members, or of their neighbour Ministers, or Brethren. For there is a brotherly communion, as between the members of the same church, so between the churches. *We have a little sister* (says one church to another Song of Solomon 8:8) therefore churches have a brotherly communion amongst themselves. Look then as one brother being offended with

another, and not able to heal him by the mouth of two or three Brethren privately, it behoves him to carry it to the whole church; for by proportion, if one church see matter of offence in another, and be not able to heal it in a more private way, it will behove them to procure the Assembly of many churches, that the offence may be orderly heard, and judged and removed.

3. It may so fall out, that the state of all the churches in the country may be corrupted; and beginning to discern their corruption, may desire the concurse and counsel of one another, for a speedy and safe, and general reformation. And then so meeting and conferring together, may renew their covenant with God, and conclude and determine upon a course that may tend to the public healing, and salvation of them all. This was a frequent practice in the Old Testament, in the time of *Asa* (2 Chronicles 15:10-15). In the time of *Hezekiah* (2 Chronicles 29:4-19). In the time of *Josiah* (2 Chronicles 34:29-33). And in the time of *Ezra* (Ezra 10:1-5). These and the like examples were not peculiar to the Israelites, as one entire *national Church*: For in that respect they appealed from every *Synagogue* and Court in *Israel*, to the *national high Priest, and* Court at *Jerusalem*, as being all of them subordinate thereunto (and therefore that precedent is usually waved by our best Divines, as not applicable to Christian churches): but these examples hold forth no superiority in one church or court over another, but all of them in an equal manner, give advice in common, and take one common course for redress of all. And therefore such examples are fit precedents for churches of equal power within themselves, to assemble together, and take order with one accord, for the reformation of them all.

Now a Synod being assembled; three questions arise about their power: 1. *What* is that *power* they have received? 2. How far the *fraternity concurs* with the Presbytery in it: the brotherhood with the Eldership? 3. Whether the power they have received reaches to the enjoining of things, both in their nature, and in their use different?

For the first, we dare not say that their power reaches no farther than giving counsel: for such as their ends be, for which according to God, they do assemble, such is the power given them of God, as may attain those ends. As they meet to minister light and peace to such churches, as through want of light and peace lie in error (or doubt at least) and variance; for they have power by the grace of Christ, not only to give light and counsel in matter of Truth and Practice; but also to command and enjoin the things to be believed and done. The express words of the Synod's letter imply no less; *it seemed good to the Holy Ghost, and unto us, to lay upon you no other burden* (Acts 15:28). This burden, therefore, to observe those necessary things, which they speak of, they, had power to impose. It is an act of the binding power of the keys, to *bind burdens.* And this *binding power* arises not only *materially* from the weight of the matters imposed, (which are necessary *necessitate praecepti* from the word) but also *formally,* from the authority of the Synod, which being an Ordinance of Christ, binds the more for the Synods sake. As a truth of the Gospel taught by a Minister of the Gospel, but also because a Minister for his calling's sake teaches it, seeing Christ has said, *who receiveth you receiveth me.* And also feeling a Synod sometime meets to convince and *admonish* an offending church or Presbytery; they have *power* therefore, (if they cannot heal the offenders) to *determine to withdraw communion from them.* And further, seeing they meet likewise sometimes for general reformation; they have power to *decree* and publish such *Ordinances,* as may conduce according to God, unto such Reformation: Examples whereof we read (Nehemiah 10:32-39; 2 Chronicles 15:2-3).

For the second question, how far the *Fraternity,* or the *Brethren* of the church, may *concur* with the *Elders* in exercising the power of the Synod?

The Answer is: The power, which they have received; is a power of liberty. As 1. They have liberty to *dispute their doubts* modestly and Christianly among the *Elders*: For in that Synod at *Jerusalem,* as there was *much disputation* (Acts 15:7) so the *multitude* had part in the *Disputation verse* 12. For after *Peter's* Speech, it is said, *the whole multitude kept silence,* and silence from what? *To know,* from the speech last in hand amongst them, and that was, from *Disputation.* 2. The *Brethren* of the church had liberty to join with the *Apostles* and *Elders*, in approving of the *sentence of James,* and *determining* the same as the common sentence of them all. 3. They had liberty to join with the *Apostles* and *Elders*, in *choosing* and *sending messengers,* and in *writing Synodical* Letters in the names of all, for the publishing of the sentence of the

Synod. Both these points are expressed in the Text *verses* 22-29. Then it pleased *the Apostles and Elders, with the whole Church, to send chosen men, and to write Letters by them.* See the whole church distinguished from the *Apostles* and *Elders;* and those whom he called the *whole Church verse* 22, he calls *the Brethren verse* 23. *The Apostles, and Elders, and Brethren.*

But though it may not be denied, that the *Brethren* of the church present in the Synod, had all this power of liberty, to join with the *Apostles* and *Elders* in all these acts of the Synod; yet the *authority of the Decree* lay chiefly (if not only) in the *Apostles* and *Elders*. And therefore it is said (Acts 16:4). *That* Paul and Silas *delivered to the churches for to keep the Decrees that were ordained of the Apostles and Elders:* So then it will be most safe to preserve to the Church of *Brethren* their due liberties, and to reserve to the *Elders* their due authority.

If it were said, the *Elders* assembled in a Synod, have no authority to determine or conclude any act that shall bind the churches, but according to the instructions which before they have received from the churches.

Answer. We do not so apprehend it; for what need churches send to a Synod for light and direction in ways of truth and peace, if they were resolved aforehand how far they will go? It is true, if the *Elders* of churches shall conclude in a Synod any thing prejudicial to the Truth and Peace of the Gospel, they may justly expostulate with them at their return, and refuse such sanctions, as the Lord has not sanctioned. But if the *Elders* to be gathered in the name of Christ in a Synod, and proceed according to the rule (the word) of Christ, they may consider and conclude sundry points expedient for the estate of their Churches, which the Churches were either ignorant or doubtful of before.

As for the third question, whether the Synod has power to enjoin such things as are both in their nature and their rule indifferent? We should answer it negatively, and our reasons are:

1. From the pattern of that precedent of Synods (Acts 15:28). They laid upon the Churches no *other burden* but those *necessary things*:

necessary, though not all of them in their own nature, yet for present use, to *avoid the offence* both of *Jew* and *Gentile*: of the *Jew*, by *eating things strangled, and blood*; of the *Gentile* and *Jew* both, by *eating things sacrificed to Idols*, as *Paul* expounds that *Article* of the Synod (1 Corinthians 8:10-12; 10:28). This eating with offence was a murder of a weak brother's soul, and a sin against Christ (1 Corinthians 8:11-12) and therefore necessary to be forborne, *necessitate praecepti*, by the necessity of God's Commandment.

2. A second reason may be, from the latitude of the Apostolicall commission, which was given to them (Matthew 28:19-20), where the Apostles are commanded to *teach the people to observe all things, which Christ had commanded.* If then the Apostles teach the people to observe more than Christ had commanded, they go beyond the bounds of their commission, and a larger commission than that given to the Apostles, nor Elders, nor Synods, nor Churches can challenge.

If it be said, Christ speaks only of teaching such things which he had commanded as necessary to salvation.

Answer. If the Apostles or their successors should hereupon usurp an authority to teach the people things indifferent, they must plead their authority from some other commission given them elsewhere: for in this place there is no footstep for any such power. That much urged, and much abused place in (1 Corinthians 14:40), will not reach it: for though *Paul* requiring in that place, all the duties of Gods worship, whether Prayer, or prophesying, or Psalms, or Tongues, etc, that they should be performed *decently and orderly,* he thereby forbids any performance of it undecently; as for men with long hair, and women to speak in open assemblies, especially to pray with their hair loose about them. And though he forbids also men *speaking two or three at once,* which to do, were not *order,* but *confusion;* yet he does not at all, neither himself enjoin, nor allow the Church of *Corinth* to enjoin such things as decent, whose want, or whose contrary is not undecent; nor such orders, whose want or contrary would be no disorder. Suppose the Church of Corinth, (or any other Church or Synod) should enjoin their Ministers to preach in a gown. A gown is a decent garment to preach in: yet such an Injunction is not grounded upon that Text of the Apostle. For then a Minister neglecting to preach in a gown, should neglect the commandment of the Apostle, which he does not. For if he preach in a cloak, he preaches decently enough, and that is all, which the Apostles Canon reaches to. In these things Christ never provided for *uniformity,* but only for *unity.*

For a third reason of this point, (and to add no more) it is taken from the nature of the Ministerial Office, whether in a Church or Synod. Their office is *stewardly*, not *lordly*: they are Ambassadors from Christ, and for Christ. Of a Steward it is required he be found faithful (1 Corinthians 4:1-2), and therefore may dispense no more injunctions to God's house, then Christ has appointed him: Neither may an Ambassador proceed to do any act of his office, further then what he has received in his Commission from his Prince. If he goes further, he makes himself a Prevaricator, not an Ambassador.

But if it is required, *whether a Synod has power of Ordination and Excommunication;* we should not take upon us hastily to censure the many notable precedents of ancient and later Synods, who have put forth acts of power in both these kinds. Only we doubt that *from the beginning it was not so*: And for our own parts, if any occasion of using this power should arise amongst ourselves (which hitherto, through preventing mercy, it has not) we (in a Synod) should rather choose to *determine,* and to *publish* and *declare* our determination. That the ordination of such as we find fit for it, and the excommunication of such as we find do deserve it, would be an acceptable service both to the Lord, and to his Churches: but the *administration* of both these acts we should refer to the *Presbytery* of the *several Churches*, whereto the person to be ordained is called, and whereof the person to be excommunicated is a member: and both acts to be performed in the presence, and with the consent of several Churches, to whom the matter appertains. For in the beginning of the Gospel in that precedent of Synods (Acts 15), we find the false teachers *declared* to be *disturbers* and *troublers* of the Churches, and subverters *of their souls* (Acts 15:24), but no condign (wholly worthy) censure dispensed against them by the Synod. An evident argument to us, that they left the censure of such offenders (in case they repented not) to the particular Churches, to whom they did appertain. And for Synodical ordination, although (Acts

1), be alleged where *Matthias* was called to be an Apostle, yet it does not appear that they acted then in a Synodical way, no more then the *Church of Antioch* did when with *fasting and prayer* they by their Presbyters *imposed hands* on *Paul* and *Barnabas,* and thereby *separated* them to *the work* of the Apostleship, whereto the *Holy Ghost had called them (Acts 13:1-3).* Whence as the Holy Ghost then said, Ἀφορίσατε δή μοι τὸν Βαρναβᾶν καὶ τον Σαῦλον: so thereupon *Paul* styles himself ἀπόστολος, ἀφωρισμένος **(8)** (Romans 1:1). And this was done in a particular Church, not in a Synod.

Chapter 7

Touching the first Subject of all the forementioned power of the Keys. And an explanation of Independency.

WHAT that Church is, which is the first Subject of the power of the Keys, and whether this Church have an independent power in the exercise of it, though they be made two distinct Questions, yet (if candidly interpreted) they are but one. For whatever is the first Subject of any accident or adjunct, the same is independent in the enjoyment of it, that is, in respect of deriving it from any other subject like itself. As if fire be the first subject of any power, three things occur. 1. It first receives that power of which it is the first subject and that reciprocally. 2. It first adds and puts forth the exercise of that power. 3. It first communicates that power to others. As we see in fire, which is the first subject of heat: it first receives heat and that reciprocally. All fire is hot, and whatsoever is hot is fire, or has fire in it. Again, fire first puts forth heat itself, and also first communicates heat to whatsoever things else are hot. To come then to the first subject of Church-power, or the power of the keys. The substance of the doctrine of it may be conceived and declared in a few Propositions.   Church-power is either supreme or *Sovereign,* or subordinate and *ministerial,* touching the former, take this proposition.

The Lord Jesus Christ, the *head* of his Church, is the Πρωτον Δεκτικον **(9)**, the first proper subject of the *sovereign power* of the *Keys.* He *hath the Key of David: He openeth, and no man shutteth; He shutteth, and no man openeth* (Revelation 3:7). *The government is upon his shoulders* (Isaiah 9:6). And himself declares the same to his Apostles, as the ground of his granting to them Apostolicall power. *All power* (says he) *is given to me in heaven and earth* (Matthew 28:18) *go therefore*, etc.

Hence 1. *All legislative power* (power of making Laws) in the church is in him, and not from him derived to any other (James 4:12; Isaiah 33:22). The power derived to others, is only to publish and execute his Laws and

Ordinances, and to see them observed (Matthew 28:20). *His Laws are perfect* (Psalm 19:9) and do *make the man of God perfect* to every *good work* (2 Timothy 3:17) and need no addition.

2. From his sovereign power it proceeds, that he only can erect and ordain a true constitution of a Church estate, (Hebrews 3:3-6). *He buildeth his own house*, and sets the pattern of it, as God gave to *David* the pattern of *Solomon's* Temple (1 Chronicles 28:19). None has power to erect any other Church-frame, then as this Master-builder has left us a pattern of it in the Gospel. In the Old Testament, the *Church* set up by him, was *National*, in the New, *Congregational*; Yet so as that in sundry cases it is ordered by him, many Congregations or their Messengers, may be assembled into a Synod (Acts 15).

3. It is from the same sovereign power, that all the offices, or ministers in the Church, are ordained by him (1 Corinthians 12:5) yes and all the *members are set in the body by him,* together with all the power belonging to their offices and places: as in the natural body, so in the Church (1 Corinthians 12:18).

4. From this sovereign power in like sort it is, that all gifts to discharge any office, by the officers, or any duty by the members, are from him (1 Corinthians 12:11). All *treasures of wisdom,* and knowledge, and grace, and the fullness of it, are in him for that end (Colossians 2:3, 9-10; John 1:16).

From this sovereign power it is, that all the spiritual power, and efficacy, and blessing, in the administration of these gifts in these offices and places, for the gathering and edifying, and perfecting of all the Churches, and all the Saints in them, are from him (Matthew 28:20), *Lo I am with you always, etc,* (Colossians 1:29; 1 Corinthians 15:9).

The good pleasure of the Father, the personal union of the human nature with the eternal Son of God, his purchase of his Church with his own blood, and his deep humiliation of himself unto the death of the Cross, have all of them obtained to him this his highest exaltation, to be *head over all things unto the Church*, and to enjoy as king of it this sovereign power (Colossians 1:19; 2:9-10; Acts 20:28; Philippians 2:8-11).

But of this sovereign power of Christ, there is no question amongst *Protestants,* especially studious of Reformation. Now as concerning the *Ministerial* power, we give these following *Propositions*.

1. *Proposition. A particular Church or congregation of Saints, professing the faith, TAKEN INDEPENDENTLY FOR ANY CHURCH* (one as well as another) *is the first subject of all the Church-offices, with all their spiritual gifts and power,* which Christ has given to be executed amongst them; *whether it be* Paul, *or* Appollos, *or* Cephas, *all are yours,* (speaking to the Church of *Corinth,* 1 Corinthians 3:22). Not as a peculiar privilege unto them, but common to them, with any other particular church; And theirs was such a church, of whom it is said, *that they came all together into one place,* for the communication of their spiritual gifts (1 Corinthians 14:23). And *Paul* tells the same church, that *God hath set the officers,* and their gifts, and all variety of members, and their Functions *in his Church* (1 Corinthians 14:28), where it is not so well translated (*Some*) God has *set some* in his church; for he has set all; but speaking of the members of the church *verse* 27, he proceeds to exemplify those members in *verse* 28. καὶ οὐ μέν ἔθετο ὁ θεό ἐν τη ἐκκλησία, *and which God hath set in his Church;* that is, which members, *Apostles Prophets, etc.* For though the Relative be not of the same gender with the Antecedent before, yet it is an unusual thing with the Pen-men of the New Testament, to respect the sense of the words, and so the person intended, rather than the gender of their name, and to render the Relative of the same gender and case with the Substantive following: so here , οὐ μέν Ἀποσόλου Προφήτα etc **(10)**.

In the New Testament, it is not a new observation that we never read of any national church, nor of any national officers given to them by Christ. In the Old Testament indeed, we read of a National church. All the tribes of *Israel* were three times in a year to appear before the Lord in *Jerusalem* (Deuteronomy 16:16). And he appointed them there an high Priest of the whole nation, and certain solemn sacrifices by him to be administered (Leviticus 16:1-29) and together with him other Priests and Elders, and Judges, to whom all appeals should be brought, and who should judge all difficult and transcendent cases (Deuteronomy 17:8-11), but we read of no such national church or high Priest, or court in the New

Testament; And yet we willingly grant that particular churches of equal power, may in some cases appointed by Christ, meet together by themselves or by their messengers in a Synod, and may perform sundry acts of power there, as has been showed above. But the officers themselves, and all the power they put forth, they are all of them *primarily* given to the several churches of particular Congregations, either as the first subject in whom they are resident, or as the first object about whom they are conversant, and for whose sake they are gathered and employed.

II. *Proposition. The Apostles of Christ were the first subjects of Apostolic power;* Apostolical power stood chiefly in two things: First, in that each Apostle had in him all ministerial power of all the officers of the Church. They by virtue of their office, might *exhort as Pastors* (1 Timothy 2:1), *teach as Teachers* (1 Timothy 2:7), *rule as Rulers* (2 Timothy 4:1), *receive*, and *distribute* the oblations of the churches as *Deacons* (Acts 4: 35), yes, any one Apostle or Evangelist carried about with him the liberty and power of the whole church; and therefore might *baptize*; yes, and censure an offender too, as if he had the presence and concurrence of the whole Church with him. For we read that *Philip* baptized the Eunuch without the presence of any church (Acts 8:38). And that *Paul* himself excommunicated *Alexander* (1 Timothy 1:20), and it is not mentioned that he took the consent of any Church or Presbytery in it. It is true indeed, where he could have the consent and concurse of the Church and Presbytery in exercise of any act of church-power, he willingly took it, and joined with it, as in the ordination of *Timothy* (2 Timothy 1:6; 1 Timothy 4:14), and in the excommunication of the incestuous *Corinthian* (1 Corinthians 5:4-5). But when both himself and the person to be baptized, or ordained, or excommunicated, were absent and distant from all churches, the Apostles might proceed to put forth their power in the administration of any church act without them. The multitude and plenitude of power, which they received immediately from Christ, would bear them out in it. *As my Father sent me* (says Christ) *namely,* with amplitude and plenitude of sovereign power, *so send I you* (with like amplitude and plenitude of ministerial power) (John 20:21).

2. Apostolical power extended itself to all churches, as much as to anyone. *Their line went out into all the world* (Psalm 19:4, compared with Romans 10). And as they received commission to preach and baptize in all the world (Matthew 28:19). So they received charge to *feed* the flock of Christ's *Sheep and Lambs* (which implies all acts of Pastoral government over all the *Sheep* and *Lambs* of Christ) (John 21:15-17). Now this Apostolical power, centering all church-power into one man, and extending itself forth to the circumference of all churches, as the Apostles were the first subject of it, so were they also the last; Nevertheless, that ample and universal latitude of power, which was conjoined in them, is now divided even by themselves amongst all the churches, and all the officers of the churches respectively, the officers of each church attending the charge of the particular church committed to them, by virtue of their office, and yet none of them neglecting the good of other churches, so far as they may be mutually helpful to one another in the Lord.

III. *Proposition.* When the church of a particular congregation walks together in the truth and peace, the *Brethren* of the church are the *first subject of church liberty,* and the *Elders* of it of *Church-authority;* and *both* of them together are the first subject of *all church-power* needful to be exercised within themselves, whether in the election and ordination of officers, or in the censure of offenders in their own body.

Of this *Proposition* there be three *Branches:* 1. That the Brethren of a particular church of a congregation are the first subjects of church-liberty: 2. That the Elders of a particular church are the first subjects of church authority: 3. That both the Elders and Brethren, walking and joining together in truth and peace, are the first subjects of all church-power, needful to be exercised in their own body. Now that the key of church-privilege or liberty is given to the Brethren of the church, and the key of rule and authority to the Elders of the church, has been declared above, in *Chapter* 3. But that these are the first subjects of these keys; and first the church, the first subject of liberty, may appear thus.

From the removal of any former subject of this power or liberty, from whence they might derive it. If the Brethren of the Congregation were not the first subjects of their church-liberty, then they derived it either from their own Elders, or from other Churches. But they derived it not from their own Elders: for they had power and liberty to choose their own Elders has been showed above, and therefore they had this liberty before they had Elders, and so could not derive it from them.

Nor did they derive it from other particular churches. For all the particular churches are of equal liberty and power within themselves, not one of them subordinate to another. We read not in Scripture, that the Church of *Corinth* was subject to that of *Ephesus,* not that of *Ephesus* to *Corinth*; no, nor that of *Cenchrea* to *Corinth*, though it was a church situated in their vicinity. Nor did they derive their liberty from a Synod of churches. For we found no footstep in the pattern of Synods (Acts 15), that the Church of *Antioch* borrowed any of their liberties from the Synod at *Jerusalem*. They borrowed indeed light from them, and decrees, tending to the establishment of truth and peace. For upon the publishing the decrees of that Synod, the Churches were established in the faith (or truth) (Acts 16:4-5), and also in consolation and peace (Acts 15:31-32), but they did not borrow from them any church-liberty at all.

2. Now the *second branch* of the *Proposition* was: That the Elders of the church of a particular Congregation, are the first subject of rule or authority, in that church (or congregation) over which the Holy Spirit has made them overseers.

1. From the charge of rule over the Church committed to them immediately from Christ: For though the Elders be chosen to their office by the church of Brethren, yet the office itself is ordained immediately by Christ, and rule annexed to the office, is limited by Christ only. If the Brethren of the church should elect a presbytery to be called by them in the Lord, this will not excuse the Presbyters in their neglect of rule, either before the Lord, or to their own consciences. For thus runs the Apostle's charge to the Elders of *Ephesus* (Acts 20:28) *Take heed to yourselves, and to the whole flock, over which the Holy Ghost hath made you overseers.*

2. The same appears from the gift of rule, required especially in an Elder, without which they are not capable of election to that office in the church (1 Timothy 3:4-5). He must be one *that is able to rule well his own house,* or else how shall he order the church of God? The like gift of rule

is not necessary to the admission of a member into the church, as to the election of an Elder: If a private brother be not so well able (through weakness in prudence or courage) to rule his own house, it will not justly debar a man from election to the office of an Elder. Neither has God given a spirit of rule and government ordinarily to the greater part of the body of the brethren: and therefore neither has given them the first Receipt of the key of Authority, to whom he has not given the gift to employ it.

If it were objected, how can the brethren of the Church invest an Elder with rule over them, if they had not power or rule in themselves to communicate to him?

Answer. They invest him with rule, partly by choosing him to the office which God has invested with rule, partly by professing their own subjection to him in the Lord: we by the rule of Relatives do necessarily infer, and prefer the authority of the Elders over them. For in yielding subjection, they either set up, or acknowledge Authority in him, to whom they yield subjection.

Objection 2. The body of the Church is the Spouse of Christ, the Lambs wife, and ought not the wife to rule the servants and stewards in the house, rather than they her? Is it not meet that the keys of Authority should hang at her girdle rather than at theirs?

Answer. There is a difference to be put between Queens, Princes, Ladies of great Honour (such as the Church is to Christ, (Psalm 45:9), and Country housewives, poor men's wives. Queens and great persons have several offices and officers for every business and service about the house, as Chamberlains, Stewards, Treasurers, Comptrollers, Ushers, Bailiffs, Grooms and Porters, who have all the authority of ordering the affairs of their Lords house in their hands. There is not a key left in the Queens hand of any office, but only of power and liberty to call for what she wants according to the Kings royal allowance: which if she exceed, the officers have power to restrain her by order from the King. But country housewives, and poor men's wives, whose husbands have no Officers, Bailiffs or Stewards, to oversee and order their estates, they may carry the keys of any office at their own girdles, which the husband

62

keeps not in his own hand. Not because poor housewives have greater authority in the house than Queens, but because of their property and mean estate, they are fain to be instead of many servants to their husbands.

Objection 3. The whole body natural, is the first subject of all the natural power of any member in the body as the faculty of sight is first in the body, before in the eye.

Answer. It is not in the mystical body (the Church) in all respects alike, as in the natural body. In the natural body there be all the faculties of each part actually inexistent, though not exerting or putting forth themselves, till each member be articulated and formed. But in the body of the Church of Brethren it is not so. All the several functions of Church-power are not actually inexistent in the body of Brethren, unless some of them have the gifts of all the officers, which often they have not, having neither Presbyters, nor men fit to be presbyters. Now if the power of the Presbytery were given to a particular Church of Brethren, as such, *primo & perse*, then it would be *found* in every particular Church of Brethren. For *a quatenus ad omnia valet consequentia* **(11)**.

Objection 4. But it is an unusual tenant in many of our best Divines that the government of the Church is mixed of a Monarchy, an Aristocracy, and a Democracy. In regard of Christ the head, the government of the Church is sovereign and monarchical. In regard of the Rule by the Presbytery, it is stewardly and Aristocratical: in regard of the people power in elections and censures, it is Democratical: which argues, the people have some stock of χράτος, power and authority in the government of the Church.

Answer. In a large sense, Authority after a sort may be acknowledged in the people. As 1. When a man acts by counsel according to his own discerning freely, he is then said to be αὐτεξαύσιος **(12)**, *Dominus sui actus*. So the people in all the acts of liberty, which they put forth, are *Domini sui actus,* Lords of their own act on.

2. The people by their acts of liberty, as in election of officers, and concurrency in censure of offenders, and in the Determination and

Promulgation of Synodical acts; they have a great stroke of power in the ordering of Church-affairs, which may be called , κράτο or *potestas,* a *Power,* which many times goes under the name of rule or authority, but in proper speech it is rather a privilege or liberty than authority, as has been opened above in *Chapter* 3. For no act of the people's power or liberty does properly bind unless the authority of the Presbytery concurre with it.

3. A third argument whereby it may appear that the Elders of a particular Church are the first subject of authority in that Church, is taken from the like removal of other subjects, from whence they might be thought to derive their authority, as was used before to prove the Church of Brethren was the first subject of their own liberty in their own Congregation. The Elders of Churches are never found in Scripture to derive their authority, which they exercise in their own Congregation, either from the Elders of other Churches, or from any Synod or Churches. All particular Churches and all Elders of them are of equal power, each of them respectively in their own congregations. None of them call others their Rabbis, or Masters, or Fathers (in respect of any authority over them) but all of them own and acknowledge one another as fellow brethren (Matthew 23:8-10).

And though in a Synod they have received power from Christ, and from his presence in the Synod, to exercise authority in imposing burdens (such as the Holy Spirit lays) upon all Churches whose Elders are present with them (Acts 15:28), (for the Apostles were Elders in all Churches) yet the Elders of every particular Church, when they walk with the brethren of their own Church in light and peace, they need not to derive from the Synod any power to impose the same, or the like burdens, upon their own Churches. For they have received a power and charge from Christ, to teach and command with all authority the whole counsel of God unto their people. And the people discerning the light of the truth delivered, and walking in peace with their Elders, they readily yield obedience to their Overseers, in whatsoever they see and hear by them commended to them from the Lord.

3. Now we come to the *third branch* of the third Proposition, which was this, that the Church of a particular congregation, Elders and Brethren

walking and joining together in truth and peace, are the first subject of all Church power, needful to be exercised within themselves, whether in the election or ordination of officers, or in the censure of offenders in their own body.

The truth of this may appear by these Arguments. 1. In point of *Ordination*. From the complete integrity of a Ministers calling (even to the satisfaction of his own and the peoples conscience) when both the Brethren and the Elders of a particular Church whereto he is called, have put forth the power, which belongs to them about him. As, when the brethren of the Church have chosen him to office, and the Presbytery of the Church have laid their hands upon him: and both of them in their several acts have due respect to the inward ministerial gifts whereunto God has furnished him: he may then look at himself as called by the holy Spirit, to exercise his talents in that office amongst them, and the people may and ought to receive him, as sent of God to them.

What defect may be found in such a call, when the brethren exercise their lawful liberty, and the Elders their lawful authority, in his ordination, and nothing more is required to the complete integrity of a Ministers calling? If it be said, there wanted imposition of hands by the Bishop, who succeeded in the place of *Timothy* and *Titus*, whom the Apostle *Paul* left, the one in Ephesus, the other in Crete, to ordain Elders in many Churches (Titus 1:5).

Answer. Touching ordination by *Timothy* and *Titus*, and upon pretence of them) by Bishops, enough has been said by many godly learned before this time, especially of later times.

The sum comes to these conclusions. 1. That *Timothy* and *Titus* did not ordain Elders in many Churches, as Bishops, but as Evangelists. *Timothy* is expressly termed an Evangelist (2 Timothy 4:5). And *Titus* is as clearly deciphered to be an Evangelist as *Timothy,* by the characters of an Evangelist, which either Scripture holds forth, or *Eusebius* notes, in his *Ecclesiastical History .lib. 3. cap 37. Gr. cap. 31. Lat.* Not to be limited to a certain Church, but to follow the Apostles, finishing their work in planting and watering Churches where they came. They did indeed ordain officers where they wanted, and exercise jurisdiction (as the Apostles did) in several Churches: yet with the rest of the Presbytery, and in the presence of the whole Church (1 Timothy 5). But for the continuance of this office of an Evangelist in the Church, there is no direction in the Epistles either to *Timothy* or *Titus*, or anywhere else in Scripture.

2. Conclusion. Those Bishops whose callings or offices in the Church, are set forth in those Epistles to be continued; they are altogether synonymous with Presbyters (Titus 1:5-7; 1 Timothy 3:1-7).

3. Conclusion. We read of many Bishops to one Church (Philippians 1:1; Acts 14:23, 20:17, 28; Titus 1:5-7), but not of many Churches (much less all the Churches in a large Diocese) to one Bishop.

4. Conclusion. There is no transcendent proper work, cut out, or reserved for such a transcendent officer as a Diocesan Bishop throughout the New Testament. The transcendent acts reserved to him by the Advocates of Episcopacy are Ordination and Jurisdiction. Now both these are acts of Rule. And *Paul* and *Timothy* acknowledge no Rulers in the Church above Pastors and Teachers, who labour in word and doctrine, but rather Pastors and Teachers above them. The Elders (says he) that rule well, are worthy of double honour, but especially they that labour in Word and Doctrine (1 Timothy 5:17).

5. Conclusion. When after the Apostles times, one of the Pastors by way of eminence was called Bishop for order sake, yet for many years he did not act of power, but 1. With consent of the Presbytery. 2. With consent, and in the presence of the people. As is noted out of *Eusebius, Ecclesiastical History, lib. 6. Ca. 43. Gr. ca. Lat. Cyprian Epistles. Lib. 3. Epistles. 10 and lib, 1. Epistle 3. Casaub. adversus Baronium, exercitat. 15. Num. 28.*

When it is alleged out of *Jerome* to confirm the same, that in the primitive times, *Communi Presbyterorum consilio, Ecclesiae gubernabantur* **(13)**. It is a weak and poor evasion, to put it off with observing, that he says, *Communi Presbyterorum consilio,* not *autboritate.* For 1. No authority is due to Presbyters over the bishop or Pastor, no more than to the Pastor over them. They are συμπρεσβύτερο fellow-Elders, and coequal in authority. And 2. When *Jerome* says, the

66

Churches were governed by the common counsel, but all with it, else it might be said, the bishop governed the Churches with the common counsel of presbyters, that is to say, asked, but not followed. And that would imply a contradiction to *Jerome's* testimony, to say the Churches were governed by the sole authority of Bishops, and yet not without asking the common counsel of the presbyters. For in asking their counsel, and not following it, the Bishop should order and govern the Churches against their counsel. Now that the churches were governed by the common counsel of Presbyters, and against the common counsel of Presbyters, are flat contradictions.

2. For a second Argument, to prove that the brethren of the Church of a particular congregation, walking with their Elders in truth and peace, are the first subject of all that church-power which is needful to be exercised in their own body: It is taken:

From their indispensable and independent power in church censures. The censure that is ratified in heaven cannot be dispensed with all, nor reversed by any power on earth. Now the censure that is administered by the Church of a particular congregation is ratified in Heaven. For so says the Lord Jesus touching the power of Church-censures (Matthew 18:17-18). If the offender refuses *to hear the church, let him be to thee as a Heathen and a Publican. Verily I say unto you, whatsoever ye shall bind on earth, shall be bound in heaven: and whatsoever ye shall loose on earth; shall be loosed in Heaven.*

Against this Argument from this Text many objections are wont to be made, but none that will hold.

Objection 1. By *Church* in (Matthew 18:17) is not meant the Christian Church (for it was not yet extant, nor could the Apostles then have understood Christ if he had so meant) but the *Jewish* church, and so he delivered their censure, in a *Jewish* phrase to account a man as *an Heathen and a Publican.*

Answer. 1. The Christian Church, though it was not then extant, yet the Apostles knew as well what he meant by *Church* in (Matthew 18:17), as they understood what he meant by *building his Church upon the Rock* in

(Matthew 16:18). It was enough the Apostles looked for a Church which Christ would gather, and build upon the confession of *Peter's* faith; and being built, should be endued with heavenly power in their censures, which they more fully understood afterwards, when having received the Holy Spirit, they came to put these things in practice.

Answer. 2. The allusion in the Church-censure to the *Jewish* custom, in accounting a man as an *Heathen* and *Publican,* does not argue that Christ directs his Disciples to complain of scandals to the *Jewish* Synagogues; but only directs them how to walk towards obstinate offenders, excommunicate by the Christian Church, namely, to walk towards them, as the *Jews* walk towards *Heathens'*, (namely, denying them religious communion) and as towards *Publicans,* withholding from them familiar civil communion; for so the *Jews* said to Christ's Disciples, *Why eateth your Master with Publicans and Sinners?*

Answer. 3. Is it not credible, that Christ would send his Disciples to make complaint of their offences to the *Jewish* Synagogues:

For, first. It is likely he would send his Lambs and Sheep, for right and healing, unto Wolves and Tigers? Both their Sanhedrin, and most of their Synagogues were no better. And if here and there some Elders of their Synagogues were better affected, yet how many it appears that, so it was, where any of themselves dwelt? And if that might appear too yet had not the *Jews* already agreed: *That if any man did confess Christ, he should be cast out the Synagogues* (John 9:22).

Objection. 2. Against the Argument from this Text, it is objected; that by the Church is meant the Bishop, or his Commissary.

Answer. 1. One man is not the Church.

If it were said, one man may represent a church; the reply is ready: one man cannot represent the Church, unless he is sent forth by the Church; but so is neither the Bishop nor his Commissary. They send not for them, but they come unsent for, (like water into a ship) chiefly for the terror of the servants of Christ, and for the encouragement of the profane. And though some of Christ's servants have found some favour from some few of Bishops, (men of more learning and ingenuity) yet those Bishops have found less favour themselves from their fellow-Bishops.

Answer. 2. The Bishop ordinarily is no member of the Church of that congregation, where the offence is committed, and what is his satisfaction to the removal of the offence given to the Church?

Answer. 3. The New Testament acknowledges no such ruler in the Church, as claims honour above Elders that labour in Word and Doctrine (1 Timothy 5:17).

Objection. 3. To tell the Church, is to tell the Presbytery of the Church.

Answer. 1. We deny not, the offence is to be told to the Presbytery; yet not to them as the Church, but as the guides of the church, who, if upon hearing the cause, and examining the witnesses, they find it right for public censure, they are then to propound it to the Church, and to try and clear the state of the cause before the church, that so the church discerning fully the nature and quality of the Elders against it, to the confusion of the offender; and the public edification of them all, who hearing and fearing, will learn to beware of the like wickedness.

Answer. 2. The Church is never put for the Presbytery alone (throughout the New Testament) though sometime it be put expressly for the Fraternity alone, as they are distinguished from the Elders and Officers (Acts 15:22) and therefore Tell the Church, cannot be meant Tell the Presbytery alone.

Objection. In the Old Testament, the Congregation is often put for the Elders and Rulers of the Congregation.

Answer. Let all the places alleged be examined, and it will appear, that in matters of judgement, where the Congregation is put for the Elders and Rulers. It is never meant (for ought we can find) of the Elders and Rulers alone, sitting apart, and retired from the Congregation; but sitting in the presence of the Congregation, and hearing and judging causes before them: In which case, if a sentence has passed from a Ruler, with the dislike of the Congregation, they have not stuck to show their dislike of the Congregation, they have not stuck to show their dislike, sometime by protesting openly against it (as 1 Samuel 14:44-45) sometime by refusing to execute it (1 Samuel 20:16-17). And what the people of the Congregation lawfully did in some cases, at sometimes, in waving and counterpoising the sentence of their Rulers, the same they might and ought to have done in the like cases at any time. The whole Host or Congregation of *Israel* might protest against an unrighteous illegal sentence; and a part of the Congregation, who discerned the iniquity of a sentence, might justly withdraw themselves from the execution of it.

Objection. 4. When Christ said *Tell the Church*, he meant Synodical or Classical Assembly of the Presbyters of many Churches. For it was his meaning and purpose in this place, to prescribe a rule for the removing of all scandals out of the Church, which cannot be done by telling the Church of one Congregation; for what if an Elder offend; yes, what if the whole Presbytery offend? The people or brethren have not power to judge their Judges, to rule their Rulers. Yes, what if the whole Congregation fall under an offence (as they may do, Leviticus 4:13) a Synod of many Presbyters may reform them, but so cannot any one Congregation alone; if the Congregation that gave the offence stand in it.

Answer. 1. Reserving due honour to Synods rightly ordered, or (which is all one) a *Classic* or *Convention* of Presbyters of particular churches, we do not find that a Church is any where put for a Synod of Presbyteries. And it were very incongruous in this place: For though it be said a particular Congregation cannot reach the removal of all offences; so it may be as truly said, that it were unsuitable to trouble Synods with every offence that falls out in a Congregation; Offences fall out often, Synods meet but seldom; and when they do meet, they find many more weighty employments. Then to attend to every offence of every private brother. Besides, as an whole particular Congregation may offend, so may a general Assembly of all the Presbyters in a Nation offend also: For general Councils have erred; and what remedy shall be found to remove such errors and offences out of this Text? Moreover, if an offence be found in a Brother of a Congregation, and the Congregation be found faithful and willing to remove it by due censure; why should the offence be called up to a more public judicature, and the plaster made broader than the sore?

Again, if an Elder offends, the rest of the Presbytery with the Congregation joining together may proceed against him, (if they cannot otherwise heal him) and so remove the offence from amongst them. If the whole Presbytery offend, or such a part as will draw a party and a faction in the Church with them, their readiest course is, to bring the matter then to a Synod. For though this place in *Matthew* direct not to that; yet the Holy Spirit leaves us not without direction in such a case but gives us a pattern in the church of *Antioch*, to repair to a Synod. And the like course is to be taken in the offence of a whole Congregation if it were persisted in with obstinacy. Neither is it true which was said, that it was the purpose of Christ in (Matthew 18:17) to prescribe a rule for the removal of all offences out of the Church; but only of such private and less heinous offences, as grow public and notorious only by obstinacy of the offenders: For if offences be heinous and public at first, the Holy Spirit does not direct us to proceed in such general course from a private admonition by one brother alone, and then to a second, by one or two more, and at last, to tell it to the Church. But in such a case the Apostles give another rule (1 Corinthians 5:11) to cast a heinous notorious offender, both out of church-communion, and private familiar communion also.

Objection. 5. The Church here spoken of (Matthew 18:17) is such a one, as whereto a complaint may orderly be made: But a complaint cannot be orderly made to a multitude, such as a whole Congregation is.

Answer. And why may not a complaint be orderly made to a whole multitude? The *Levite* made an orderly complaint to a greater multitude, than four hundred particular Congregations are wont to amount to (Judges 20:1-4, etc).

Objection. 6. The Church here to be complained of meets with authority, (for censures are administered with authority) but the church of a particular Congregation meets with humility, to seek the face and favour of God.

Answer. Humility to God may well stand with authority to men. The twenty four Elders (who represent the grown hairs of the Church of the New Testament) they are said in Church-assemblies to sit up on thrones with crowns on their heads (Revelation 4:4) yet when they fall down to worship God and the Lamb; they cast down their crowns at his feet *verse 10.*

Objection. 7. In the church of a particular Congregation, a woman may not speak: but in this Church here spoken of, they may speak; for they may be offenders, and offenders must give an account of their offences.

Answer. When the Apostle forbids women to speak in the church, he means, speaking partly by way of authority, as in public praying or prophesying in the Church (1 Timothy 2:2) partly by way of bold inquiry, in asking questions publicly of the Prophets in the face of the Church (1 Corinthians 14:34). But to answer it: If the whole Congregation have taken just offence at the open sin of a woman, she is bound as much to give satisfaction to the whole Congregation, as well as to the Presbytery.

Objection. 8. When Schisms grew to be scandalous in the Church of *Corinth*, the household of *Chloe* told not the whole Congregation of it, but *Paul* (1 Corinthians 1:11).

Answer. The contentions in the Church of *Corinth* were not the offence of a private brother, but of the whole church. And who can tell whether they had not spoken of it to the Church before? But whether they had or not, the example only argues, that Brethren offended with the sins of their brethren, may tell an Elder of the Church of it, that he may tell it to the Church, which no man denies. *Paul* was an Elder of every church of Christ, as the other Apostles were, as having the government of all the churches committed to them all.

Having thus (by the help of Christ) cleared this Text in (Matthew 18:17) from a variety of misconstructions, (which not, the obscurity of the words, but the eminency of the gifts, and worth of Expositors has made difficult). Let us add an argument or two more to the same purpose, to prove, that the Church of a particular Congregation, fully furnished with officers, and rightly walking in judgement and peace, is the first subject of all Church-authority, needful to be exercised within their own body.

3. A third argument to prove this is usually and justly taken from the practice and example of the Church of *Corinth*, in the excommunication of the incestuous *Corinthian* (1 Corinthians 5:1-5).

Objection. 1. The excommunication of the incestuous *Corinthian*, was not an act of judicial authority in the church of *Corinth*, whether Elders or Brethren, but rather an act of subjection to the Apostle, publishing the sentence, which the Apostle had before decreed and judged: for (says the Apostle) I though absent in body, yet present in spirit, have judged already, concerning him that has done this deed, etc.

Answer. 1. Though *Paul* (as a chief Officer of every church) judged before-hand the excommunication of the incestuous *Corinthian*: yet his judgement was not a judicial sentence, delivering him to Satan, but a judicious doctrine and instruction, teaching the Church what they ought to do in that case.

2. The act of the church in *Corinth* in censuring the incestuous person, was indeed an act of subjection to the Apostles divine doctrine and direction (as all church-censure, by whomsoever administered, ought to be acts of subjection to the word of Christ) but yet their act was a complete act of just power, (even an act of all that liberty and authority which is to be put forth in any censure). For, first they delivered him to Satan, in the name of the Lord Jesus, *verse* 4 and that is the highest power in the Church. Secondly, the spirit of *Paul*, that is, his Apostolic spirit was gathered together with them, in delivering and publishing sentence, which argues, both his power and theirs was coincident and concurrent in this sentence. Thirdly, the holy end and life of this sentence argues the heavenly power from whence it proceeded. They delivered him to Satan for the destruction of the flesh (that is, for the mortifying of his corruption) that his soul might be saved in the day of the Lord Jesus. Fourthly, when his soul came to be humble and penitent by the means of this sentence, *Paul* entreats the church to release and forgive him (2 Corinthians 2:6-10). Now *ejusdem potestatis est ligare et solvere, claudere et aperire* **(14)**.

Objection. 2. All this argues no more, but that some in the church of *Corinth* had this power (that is to say, the Presbytery of the church, but no the whole body of the people) to excommunicate the offender.

Answer. 1. If the Presbytery alone had put forth this power, yet it suffices to make good the Proposition, that every church furnished with a Presbytery, and proceeding righteously and peaceably, they have within themselves so much power as it requisite, to be exercised within their own body.

Answer. 2. It is apparent by the Text that the Brethren concurred also in this sentence, and with *some act of power*, that is to say, such power as the want of putting it forth, retarded the sentence, and putting of it forth was requisite to the administration of the sentence. For, first, the reproof for not proceeding to sentence sooner is directed to the whole church, as well as to the Presbytery; *they are all blamed for not mourning, for not putting him away, for being puffed up rather* (1 Corinthians 5:2).

2. The commandment is directed to them all, *when they are gathered together,* (and what is that but to a Church meeting?) to proceed against him (1 Corinthians 5:4). In like sort, in the end of the Chapter he commands them all, *put away therefore from among you that wicked person, verse* 13.

3. He declares this act of theirs in putting him out, to be a judicial act *verse* 12. *Do you not judge them that are within?* Say that the judgement of authority be proper only to the Presbytery, yet the judgement of direction (which as concurring in this act with the Presbytery) has power in it (as was said) may not be denied to the Brethren: for here is an act of judgement ascribed to them all: which judgement in the Brethren he esteems of it so highly, that from thence he takes occasion to advise the members of the Church, to refer their differences even in civil matters, to the judgement of the Saints or Brethren, *know ye not* (says he) that *the Saints shall judge the world, yea the Angels?* (1 Corinthians 6:1-3) how much more the things of this life? Yes rather than they should go to law, and that before Infidels, in any case depending between Brethren, he advises them rather to set up the means in the Church to hear and judge between them (1 Corinthians 6:4).

4. When the Apostle directs them upon the repentance of an offender, to forgive him (2 Corinthians 2:4-10) he speaks to the Brethren, as well as to their Elders to *forgive him*. As they were all (the Brethren as well as the Elders) offended with his sin: so it was proper they should all alike be satisfied, and being satisfied should forgive him; the Brethren in a way of brotherly love and Church-consent, as well as the Elders, by sentencing his absolution and restitution to the Church.

Objection. 3. But was not this Church of *Corinth* (who had all this power) a *metropolis, a mother Church of Achaia,* in which many Presbyteries, from many Churches in the villages were assembled to administer this censure?

Answer. No such thing appears from the story of the church of *Corinth,* neither in the Acts (Acts 18), nor from either of the Epistles to the *Corinthians.* True it is, *Corinth* was a *mother-city,* but not a *mother-Church* to all *Achaia*: and yet it is not unlikely that other Churches in that region, might borrow much light from their gifts; for they abounded, and were *enriched with* variety of all *gifts* (1 Corinthians 5:7). But yet that which the Apostle calls the *Church of Corinth*, even the *whole Church* was no larger, then was wont to *meet together in one place, one congregation* (1 Corinthians 14:23).

A fourth and last *Argument* to prove the *Proposition*, that every Church so furnished with officers (as has been said) and so carried on in truth and peace, has all Church power needful to be exercised within themselves, is taken from the guilt of offence, which lies upon every Church, when any offence committed by their members lies uncensored and unmoved. Christ has something against the *Church of Pergamus,* for *suffering Balaam* and the *Nicolaitians* (Revelation 2:14-15) and something against the *Church of Thyatira*, for *suffering Jezebel.* Now if these Churches had not either of them sufficient power to purge out their own offenders, why are they blamed for toleration of them? Yes, why are not the neighbour Churches blamed for the sins of these Churches? But we see, neither is *Pergamus* blamed for tolerating *Jezebel,* nor *Thyatira* for tolerating *Balaam,* or *Smyrna* for tolerating either. Indeed what Christ writes to any one Church, his *Spirit* calls *all the Churches* to hearken unto, and so he does our Churches also at this day:

75

not because he would have them beware of the like remissness in tolerating the like offences amongst their Sister-Churches, and with brotherly love and faithfulness to admonish them of that.

It is an unfound body that wants strength to purge out his own vicious and malignant humours. And every Church of a particular congregation, being a body, even a body of Christ in itself, it were not for the honour of Christ, nor of his body, if when it were in a sound and athletic constitution, it should not have power to purge itself of its own superfluous and noisome humours.

IV. Proposition. *In case a particular Church be disturbed with error or scandal, and the same maintained by a faction* amongst them. *Now a Synod of Churches, or of their messengers, is the first subject of that power and authority, whereby error is judicially convinced and condemned, the truth searched out,* and determined, and the way of truth and peace declared and imposed upon the Churches.

The truth of this Proposition may appear by *two Arguments.*

1. *Argument.* From want of power in such a particular church to pass a binding sentence, where error or scandal is maintained by a faction; for the promise of binding and loosing which is made to a particular church (Matthew 18:18) is not given to the church, when it is leavened with error and variance. It is a received Maxine, *Clavis errans non ligat*; and it is as true, *Ecclesia litigans non ligat* **(15)**: And the ground of both arises from the estate of the Church, to which the promise of binding and loosing is made (Matthew 18:17-18) which, though it be a particular church (as has been showed) yet it is *a Church* AGREEING *together in the name of Christ* (Matthew 18:19-20). *If there want agreement amongst them, the promise of binding and loosing is not given to them:* or if they should agree in the name of Christ. For to meet in the name of Christ, implies, they meet not only by his command and authority, but also that they proceed according to his Laws and Will, and that to his service and glory. If then the church, or a considerable part of it falls into error through ignorance, or into faction by variance, they cannot expect the presence of Christ with them, according to his promise to pass a binding sentence. And then as they fall under the conviction and admonition of

76

any other sister church, in a way of brotherly love, by virtue of communion of churches; so they are errors and variance, and whatsoever scandals else do accompany the same. They are justly subject to the condemnation of a Synod of Churches.

2. A second Argument to prove that a Synod is the first subject of power, to determine and judge errors and variances in particular churches, is taken from the pattern set before us in that case (Acts 15:1-28). When certain false Teachers, having taught in the church of *Antioch*, a necessity of circumcision to salvation, and having gotten a faction to take part with them, (as appears by the στάσις and συζήτησις **(16)** of *Paul* and *Barnabas* against them) the church did not determine the case themselves, but referred the whole matter to the *Apostles* and *Elders* at *Jerusalem* (Acts 15:1-2). Not to the *Apostles* alone, but to the *Apostles* and *Elders*. The Apostles were as the Elders and Rulers of all churches; and the Elders there were not a few, the Believers in *Jerusalem* being many thousands. Neither did the Apostles determine the matter (as has been said) by Apostolical authority from immediate revelation, but they assembled together with the Elders, to *consider of the matter, verse* 6, and *a multitude of Brethren* together with them (*verses* 12, 22-23) and after, searching out the cause by an ordinary means of *disputation, verse* 7. *Peter* cleared it by the witness of the Spirit to his Ministry in *Cornelius* his family. *Paul* and *Barnabas* by the like effect of their Ministry among the *Gentiles*: *James* confirmed the same by the testimony of the *Prophets*, wherewith the whole Synod being satisfied, they determine of a judicial sentence, and of a way to publish it by letters and messengers; in which they *censure the false Teachers, as troublers of their Church, and Subverters of their souls;* they reject the imposition of *circumcision, as a yoke which neither they nor their Fathers were able to bear;* they impose upon the Churches none but some *necessary* observations, and them by way of that authority which the Lord had given them, *verse* 28. Which pattern clearly shows to us whom the *Key of Authority* is committed, when there grows offence and difference in a Church: Look as in the case of the offence of a faithful brother persisted in, the matter is at last judged and determined in a Church, which is a Congregation of the faithful; so in the case of the offence of the Church or Congregation, the

matter is at last judged in a Congregation of Churches; for what is a Synod else, but a Church of Churches?

Now, from all these former *Propositions*, which tend to clear the *first subject* of the power of the Keys, it may be easy to deduce certain *corollaries* from there, tending to clear a parallel Question to this; that is to say, *In what sense it may and ought to be admitted, that a Church of a particular congregation, is independent in the use of the power of the Keys, and in what sense not?* For in what sense the Church of a particular congregation is the first subject of the power of the keys, in the same sense it is independent, and in none other. We take the first subject and the independent subject to be all one.

1. *Corollary.* The Church is not independent on Christ, but dependant on him for all Church-power.

The reason is plain, because he is the first subject of all Church-power, by way of sovereign eminency, as has been said. And therefore the Church, and all the offices of it; yes and a Synod of Churches, is dependant upon him, for all Ministerial Church-power. *Ministry is dependant upon sovereignty*; yes, the more dependant they be upon Christ, in all the exercise of their Church power, the more powerful is all their power in all their administrations.

2. *Corollary.* The first subject of the ministerial power of the keys, though it is independent in respect of derivation of power from the power of the Sword to the performance of any spiritual administration, yet it is subject to the power of the sword in matters, which concern the civil peace.

The matters, which concern the civil peace, wherein Church-subjection is chiefly attended, are of four sorts.

1. The first sort is *civil matters,* τά βιοτιχά, the *things of this life,* as is the disposing of men's goods, or lands, lives, or liberties, tributes, customs, worldly honours, and inheritances. In these the Church submits and refers itself to the civil State. Christ as minister of the circumcision, refused to take upon him the dividing of inheritances amongst brethren, as impertinent to his calling (Luke 12:13-14). *His Kingdom* (he

78

acknowledges) *is not of this world* (John 18:36). Himself paid tribute to *Caesar* (Matthew 17:27) for himself and his Disciples.

2. The second sort of things, which concern civil peace, is the *establishment of pure religion, in doctrine, worship, and government,* according to the word of God: as also the reformation of all corruptions in any of these. On this ground the good Kings of Judah commanded *Judah to seek the Lord God of their fathers,* and to worship him, according to his own statutes and commandments: and the contrary corruptions of strange gods, high places, Images, and Groves, they removed, and are commanded of God, and obeyed by the Priests and people in so doing (2 Chronicles 14:3-5; 15:8-16; 17:6-9; 19:3-4; 24:4-6, 8-10; 29:3-35; 30:1-12; 34:3-33). The establishment of pure Religion, and the reformation of corruptions in Religion, does much concern the civil peace. If Religion be corrupted, there will be *war in the gates* (Judges 5:8) and *no peace to him that commeth in, or goeth out,* (2 Chronicles 15:3, 5-6). But where religion rejoices, the civil State flourishes (Haggai 2:15-19). It is true, the establishment of pure religion, and reformation of corruptions, pertain also to the Churches and Synodical Assemblies. But they go about it only with spiritual weapons, ministry of the Word, and Church-censures upon such as are under Church-power. But the Magistrates address themselves thereto, partly by commanding and stirring up the Churches and Ministers of it to go about it in their spiritual way: partly also by civil punishments upon the wilful opposers and distributors of the same. As Jehoshaphat *sent* Priests *and Levites,* (and them accompanied and countenanced with *Princes* and *Nobles*) *to preach and teach in the cities of Judah* (2 Chronicles 17:7-9). So *Josiah* put to death the idolatrous Priests of the high places (2 Kings 22:20). Nor was that a peculiar duty or privilege of the Kings of *Judah,* but attended to also by heathen Princes, and to prevent the wrath of God against the Realm of the *King and his sons* (Ezra 7:23). Yes, and of the times of the New Testament it is prophesied that in some cases, capital punishment shall proceed against *false prophets*, and that by the procurement of their *nearest kindred* (Zechariah 13:3). And the execution of it is described (Revelation 16:4-7) where the *rivers and fountains of waters* (that is, the Priests and Jesuits, that convey the Religion of the Sea of

Rome throughout the countries) *are turned to blood*, that is, have *blood given them to drink* by the civil Magistrate.

Nevertheless, though we willingly acknowledge a power in the civil magistrate to establish and reform Religion, according to the word of God; yet we would not be so understood, as if we judged it to belong to the civil power, to compel all men to come and sit down at the Lords table, or to enter into the communion of the Church, before they be in some measure prepared of God for such fellowship. For this is not a *Reformation*, but a *Deformation* of the Church, and is not according to the word of God, but against it, as we shall show (God willing) in the sequel, when we come to speak of the disposition or qualification of Church-members.

3. There is a third sort of things which concern the civil peace, wherein the Church is not to refuse spiritual administrations, which may advance and help forward the public good of Civil State according to God. In time of war, or pestilence, or any public calamity or danger lying upon a Commonwealth, the Magistrate may lawfully proclaim a Fast, as *Jehosophat* did (2 Chronicles 20:3) and the Churches ought not to neglect such an administration, upon such a just occasion. Neither does it impeach the power of the Church to call a Fast, when they see God calling them to public humiliation. For as *Jehosophat* called a Fast: so the Prophet *Joel* stirs up the Priests to call a Fast in time of a Famine, threatening the want of holy sacrifices (Joel 1:13-4).

It may fall out also, that in understanding a war, or in making a league with a foreign state, there may arise such cases of conscience, as may require the consultation of a Synod. In which case, or the like, if the Magistrate calls a Synod; the Churches are to yield him ready subjection herein in the Lord. *Jehosophat* though he was out of his place, when he was in *Samaria* visiting an idolatrous King: yet, he was not out of his way, when in case of undertaking the war against *Syria*, he called for counsel from the mouth of the Lord, by a Counsel or Synod of Priests and Prophets (1 Kings 22:5-7).

4. A fourth sort of things, wherein the Church is not to refuse subjection to the civil *Magistrate*, is in-patient suffering their unjust perfections

without hostile or rebellious resistance. For though persecution of the Churches and servants of Christ, will not advance the civil peace, but overthrow it; yet for the Church to take up the Sword in her own defence, is not a lawful means of preserving the Church-peace, but a disturbance of it rather. In this case, when *Peter* drew his Sword in defence of his master, (*the Lord Jesus*) against an attachment served upon him, by the officers of the high Priests and Elders of the people: our Saviour bade him *put up his sword into his sheath again;* for (says he) *all they that take the sword, shall perish by the sword* (Matthew 27:50-52) where he speaks of *Peter* either as a private Disciple, or a Church-officer, to whom, though the power of the keys was committed, yet the power of the sword was not committed. And for such to take up the sword, though in the cause of Christ, it is forbidden by Christ: and such is the case of any particular Church, or of a Synod of Churches. As they have received the power of the keys, not of the sword, so the power of the keys they may, and ought to administer, but not of the sword. Wherein nevertheless we speak of Churches and Synods, as such, that is, as church-members, or church-assemblies, acting in a church way, by the power of the keys received from Christ. But if some of the same persons be also trusted by the civil State, with the preservation and protection of the Laws and Liberties, peace and safety of the same state, and shall meet together in a public civil Assembly (whether in Council or Camp) they may there provide by civil power (according to the wholesome Laws and Liberties of the country) *Ne quid Ecclesis, ne quid Respublica detrimenti capiat* (17). If King *Saul* swear to put *Jonathan* to death, the Leaders of the people may by strong hands rescue him from his fathers unjust and illegal fury (1 Samuel 14:44-45). But if *Saul* persecutes *David*, (though as unjustly as *Jonathan*) yet if the Princes and leaders of the people will not rescue him from the wrath of the King, *David* (a private man) will not draw out his sword in his own defence, so much as to *touch the Lords anointed* (1 Samuel 24:4-7).

To conclude this *Corollary*, touching the subjection of Churches to the civil State, in matters, which concern the civil peace, this may not be omitted, that as the Church is subject to the sword of the magistrate in things which concern the civil peace; so the Magistrate (if Christian) is subject to the keys of the Church, in matters which concern the peace of his conscience, and the Kingdom of heaven. Hence it is prophesied by *Isaiah*, that Kings and Queens, who are nursing fathers and mothers to the Church, *shall bow down to the church, with their faces to the earth* (Isaiah 49:23) that is, they shall walk in professed subjection to the ordinances of Christ in his Church. Hence also it is that *David* prophesies of a *two-edge sword*, (that is, the sword of the Spirit the word of Christ, put *into the hands of the Saints* (who are by calling the members of the Church) as to subdue the Nations by the ministry of the Word, to the obedience of the Gospel (Psalm 149:6-7). So *to bind their Kings with chains and their Nobles with fetters of iron, to execute upon them the judgement written*, (that is, written in the Word) (Psalm 149:8-9).

3. A third *Corollary* touching the independency of Churches is this. That a Church of a particular Congregation consisting of Elders and Brethren, and walking in the truth and peace of the Gospel, as it is the first subject of all Church-power needful to be exercised within itself, so it is independent upon any other (Church or Synod) for the exercise of the same.

That such a Church is the first subject of all Church-power has been cleared above in the opening the third Proposition of the first subject of the power of the keys. And such a Church being the first subject of Church-power, is unavoidably independent upon any other church or body for the exercise of it; for as has been said before, the first subject of any accident or adjunct, is independent upon any other, either for the enjoying, or for the employing (the having or the using) of the same.

4. A fourth *Corollary* touching the independency of churches, is, that a Church fallen into any offence (whether it be the whole Church, or a strong party in it) is not independent in the exercise of Church-power, but is subject both to the admonition of any other Church, and to the *determination and judicial sentence* of a Synod for *direction into a way of truth and peace*. And this also arises from the former discourse. For, if *clavis errans non ligat, et Ecclesia litigans non ligat* **(18)**; that is, if Christ has not given to a particular Church a promise to bind and loose in heaven, what they bind and loose on earth, unless they agree together, and *agree in his Name*, then such a Church is not independent in their proceedings, as do fail in either. For all the independency that

can be claimed, is founded upon that promise: *What ye bind on earth, shall be bound in heaven: What ye loose on earth, shall be loosed in heaven* (Matthew 18:18). On that promise is founded both the independency and *security,* and *parity* also of all Churches. But if that promise be cut off from them, they are like *Samson* when his hair was cut of, weak, and subject to fall under other men; and yet they fall softer than he did: he fell into the hands of his enemies, but they fall under the censure of their friends. As the false Prophet recanting his error, did acknowledge, so may they: *Thus was I wounded in the house of my friends* (Zechariah 13:6). In the house of a neighbour-church or two, I was friendly smitten with a brotherly admonition, which (like *a precious oil*) did *not break mine head*: and in the house of a Synod of Churches, I was friendly, yes, brotherly censured and healed.

5. A fifth and last *Corollary* arising from the former discourse, touching the independency of Churches may be this. Though the Church of a particular Congregation, consisting of Elders and Brethren, and walking with a right foot in the truth and peace of the Gospel, be the first subject of all Church-power needful to be exercised within itself; and consequently be independent from any other Church or Synod in the use of it; yet it is a safe, and wholesome, and holy Ordinance of Christ, for such particular Churches to join together in holy Covenant communion, and consultation amongst themselves, to administer all their Church-affairs, (which are of weighty, and difficult and common concernment) not without common consultation and consent of other Churches about them. Now Church-affairs of weighty and difficult and common concernment, we account to be the *election and ordination of Elders, excommunication of an Elder,* or any *person of public note,* and employment: the *translation of an Elder* from one Church to another or the like. In which case we conceive it safe and wholesome, and an holy Ordinance, to proceed with common consultation and consent. Safe, for *in multitude of counsellors there is safety*, (as in civil, so in Church-affairs) (Proverbs 11:14). And though this or that Church may be of a good and strong constitution, and walk with a right foot in the truth, and peace of the Gospel: yet all Churches are not in a like athletic plight, and they will be loath to call in, or look out for help as much or more than others, though they have more need than others: yes, and the best_Churches

may soon degenerate, and stand in as much need of help as others, and for want of it may sink and fall into deep Apostasy, which other Churches might have prevented, had they discerned it at first.

It is also wholesome, as tending to maintain brotherly love, and fondness of doctrine in Churches, and to prevent many offences, which may grow up in this or that particular church, when it transacts all such things within itself without consent.

It is likewise an holy ordinance of Christ, as having just warrant from a like precedent. The Apostles were as much independent from one another, and stood in as little need of one another's help, as Churches do one of another. And yet *Paul* went to *Jerusalem* to confer with *Peter, James,* and *John,* lest he *should run in vain* in the course of his ministry (Galatians 2:2). And though in conference the chief Apostles added nothing to *Paul, verse* 6, yet when they perceived *the Gospel of the uncircumcision to Peter, James, and John, they gave* unto one another *the right hand of fellowship, verse* 9. Now then it will follow by just proportion, that if the Apostles, who are each of them independent one of another, had need to consult and confer together about the work of their ministry, to procure and freer passage to their calling, and to their doctrine: then surely Churches, and Elders of Churches, though independent of one another, had need to communicate their courses and proceedings in such cases one with another, to procure the freer passage to the same. And if the Apostles giving right hand of fellowship one to another, did mutually strengthen their hands in the work of the ministry: then the Elders of Churches giving right hand of fellowship to one another in their ordination, or upon any fit occasion, cannot but much encourage and strengthen the hearts and hands of one another in the Lord's work.

Again, something might be added, if not for confirmation, yet for illustration of this point, by comparing the dimensions of the *New Jerusalem,* which is a perfect platform of a pure Church, as it shall be constituted in the Jewish Church state, as their last conversion. The dimensions of this Church as they are described by *Ezekiel* (chapter 48:30) are (according to *Junius*) *twelve furlongs,* which after the measure of the Sanctuary (which is double to the common) is about *three miles* in length, and as much in breadth. But the dimensions of the same Church of the Jews, in (Revelation 21:16) is said to be *twelve thousand furlongs.* Now how can these two dimensions of the same Church stand together,

which are so far discrepant one from another? For there be a *thousand times twelve* furlongs in *twelve thousand furlongs.* The fittest and fairest reconciliation seems plainly to be this that Ezekiel speaks of the dimensions of any ordinary Jewish Church of one particular congregation. But *John* speaks of the dimensions of many particular Jewish Churches, combining together in some cases, even to the communion of a thousand Churches. Not that the Church of the Jews will be constituted in a *National* and *Diocesan* frame, with *National* officers, and *Diocesan* Bishops, or the like: but that sometimes a thousand of them will be gathered into a Synod, and all of them will have such mutual care, and yield such mutual brotherly help and communion one to another, as if they were all but one body.

If any man say, *Theologia symbolica,* or *Parabolica non est argumentativa,* that arguments from such parables, and mystical resemblances in Scripture, are not valid, let him enjoin his own apprehension: and (if he can yield a better interpretation of the place) let him wave this collection. Nevertheless, if there were no argumentative power in parables, why did the Lord Jesus so much delight in that kind of teaching? And why did *John,* and *Daniel,* and *Ezekiel,* deliver a great part of their prophecies in parables, if we must take them for riddles, and neither for documents nor arguments? Surely if they serve not for argument, they serve not for document.

But furthermore, touching this great work of communion and consociation of Churches, give us leave to add this caution; to see that this consociation of Churches be not perverted, either to the oppression or diminution of the just liberty and authority of each particular Church within itself: who being well supplied with a faithful and expert Presbytery of their own, do walk in their integrity according to the truth and peace of the Gospel. Let Synods have their just authority in all Churches, how pure so ever, in determining such Διατάξεις **(19)**, as are requisite for the edification of all Christ's Churches according to God. *But in the Election and Ordination of Officers, and Censure of Offenders, let it* *suffice the Churches consociate, to assist one another, with their counsel, and right hand of fellowship, when they see a particular Church use their liberty and power aright. But let them not put forth the power of their community, either to take such Church acts out of their hands, or to hinder them in their lawful course, unless they see them (through ignorance or weakness) to abuse their liberty and authority in the Gospel.* All the liberties of Churches were purchased to them by the precious blood of the Lord Jesus; and therefore neither may the Churches give them away, nor do many Churches take them out of the hands of one. They may indeed prevent the abuse of their liberties, and direct in the lawful use of them, but not take them away, though they should be willing. The Lord Jesus having given equal power to all the Apostles, it was not lawful for eleven of them to forbid the twelfth to do any act of his office without their intervention. Neither was it lawful for the nine, who were of inferior gifts, to commit the guidance and command of all their Apostolic administrations unto *Peter, James, and John, who seemed to be Pillars.* And that, not only because they were all (one as well as another) immediately guided by the Holy Ghost: but because they were all equal in office, and everyone to give account for himself to God.

It is the like case (in some measure) of particular Churches; yes, there is moreover a three-fold further inconvenience, which seems to us, to attend the translation of the power of particular Churches in these ordinary administrations, into the hands of a Synod of Presbyters, commonly called a *Classis.*

1. The promise of *Binding and Loosing*, in a way of Discipline, which Christ gave to every particular Church (as has been showed), is by the means not received, nor enjoined, nor practised by themselves immediately, but by their Deputies or Overseers.

2. The same promise which was not given to Synods in acts of that nature (as has been showed in the Chapter of Synods) but in acts of another kind, is hereby received and enjoined, and practised by them, and by them only, which out not to be.

And which is a third inconvenience. The practice of this power of the Keys only by a Synod of Presbyters, still keeps the Church as under nonage, as if they were not grown up to the full fruition of the just liberty of their riper years in the days of the Gospel. For a mother to bear her young daughter in her arms, and not to suffer it to go on its own feet, while it is in infancy, is kindly and comely: but when the young girl is grown up to riper years, for the mother still to bear her in her arms, for fear of stumbling, it were an unnecessary burden to the mother, and a reproach to the Virgin; such is the case here: The community of Churches (according to the Hebrew phrase) is as the Mother; each particular Church is as the *Daughter*. In the Old Testament, while the Church was in her nonage, it was not unseasonable to leave the whole guidance and bearing of it in the hands of their *Tutors and Governors, the Priests and Levites,* and in the community of the National Courts. But now in the days of the New Testament, when the Churches are grown up (or should be grown at least) to more maturity, it was suitable more to give the Church liberty to stand alone, and to walk upon her own legs; and yet in any such part of her way, as may be more hard to hit right upon, as in her Elections, and Ordinances, and Censures of eminent persons, in office; it is a safe and holy and faithful office of the vigilancy of the community of Churches, to be present with them, and helpful to them in the Lord. And at all times when a particular Church shall wander out of the way, (whether a out of the way of truth, or of peace) the community of Churches may by no means be excused from reforming them again into their right way, according to the authority which the Lord has given them for the public edification of all the several Churches within their Covenant.

Soli Christo, Τῷ Α, καί Τῷ Ω

In Christ alone, who is our Alpha and Omega

FINIS

Index

Made in the USA
Middletown, DE
08 September 2024

60530913R00051